THE VITAMIN AND MI...
SPECIAL DIET COOKBOOK

THE VITAMIN AND MINERAL SPECIAL DIET COOKBOOK

Mouthwatering recipes for maximum vitamin
and mineral power

Judy Ridgway

THORSONS PUBLISHING GROUP

First published in 1990

British Library Cataloguing in Publication Data

Ridgway, Judy
  The vitamin and mineral special diet cookbook.
  1. Recipes
  I. Title
  641.5

ISBN: 0-7225-1886-2

Published by Thorsons Publishers Limited,
Wellingborough, Northamptonshire,
NN8 2RQ, England

Typeset by Harper Phototypesetters Ltd,
Northampton, England
Printed in Great Britain by Bath Press, Bath, Avon

10 9 8 7 6 5 4 3 2 1

CONTENTS

INTRODUCTION

In today's hectic world health and vitality are of paramount importance. The modern family crams many more activities into its daily schedule than ever before. The workplace is a demanding and sometimes stressful place for most people. The majority of women go out to work but they still have to run their homes and families.

On the leisure front the emphasis is on plenty of exercise in the form of dance and keep fit classes, aerobics and gym work, jogging and cycling, not to mention the more traditional sports. Looking at the lifestyle of my family and friends it's not surprising that I sometimes feel a bit breathless!

To take advantage of all that modern life has to offer and to cope with its stresses and strains we need to keep as fit as possible. But for many people this is easier said than done. Despite the fact that in recent years the public spotlight has been focused on healthy eating with the message that we are what we eat, not everyone is clear about what this really means. Indeed the experts themselves are deeply divided. Some advocate a low-fat diet with a move from saturated fat to polyunsaturated fat. Others put more emphasis on cutting back on sugar or salt or on increasing the fibre content of what we eat. This kind of disagreement has been aggravated both by manufacturers jumping on the various bandwagons and declaring their products to be particularly healthy and by those who seem to be under attack, vigorously stating that there is nothing wrong with their products.

So what is a healthy diet?

At its simplest, a healthy diet is one which provides all the energy we need to live our lives and all the nutrients we need for growth and renewal. The body can make some of the materials it needs for body building but there are others which it cannot make. These are called essential nutrients. Essential nutrients include certain proteins and fats as well as vitamins and minerals. These must be included in the food we eat in roughly the right proportions. This is where the experts start to disagree. In the UK the current officially recommended list of essential nutrients contains 10 items. This compares with 18 in the United States and 23 in West Germany. But there are over 30 nutrients which are recognized world-wide as being essential for optimum health. The experts disagree even more markedly on the desirable levels for each of the nutrients concerned and again UK official recommendations tend to be low.

The body can get its energy from most of the food that we eat but some foods are much better sources of energy than others. Nutrients like protein, carbohydrate and fat provide quite different amounts of energy and the water content of the food will also be very relevant.

Foods which are rich in fats provide the largest amounts of energy; water rich foods like fruit and vegetables the least. Starchy foods like wholemeal bread, potatoes and pasta fall somewhere in the middle. Protein-rich foods are usually used for body building but if more are eaten than required, or there is no other energy source, they, too, will be burnt for energy.

All of these foods also provide essential nutrients. Fruit and vegetables, for example, are particularly good sources of certain vitamins and minerals, and fats contain others. The only food which contains no nutrients at all is that purest of all foods — refined sugar! However, the important thing is the way we combine foods to make up our daily diet.

Fashions in nutritional advice change with the state of scientific research, the economy of the country and the perceived state of the nation's health. Not so long ago people were being urged to eat more protein-rich foods like meat and fish and less bread and potatoes. Today the villain of the piece tends to be fat.

Current guidelines

The most generally accepted guidelines for healthy eating at the moment suggest that we should:

● Eat less fat and at the same time move some of our consumption from saturated to polyunsaturated fat. Generally speaking that means from animal to vegetable fat.

- Eat more cereals and starchy food to make up the energy lost by eating less fat.

- Eat more dietary fibre in the form of cereals and fruit and vegetables.

These guidelines are based on the belief that the intake of fat is one of the factors causing the high incidence of heart disease and other common health disorders in the West. Fibre is thought to play a part in the prevention and cure of such diseases.

Rather more controversial are the calls to cut salt and sugar consumption. The former is based on the suggestion that high-salt intake is associated with high blood-pressure. This may be true for some sections of the population and the argument runs that it would not harm any of us to cut back on the large quantities currently consumed. The arguments against sugar range from the fact that it contains no nutrients whatsoever and is bad for the teeth to the suggestion that it is sugar or sucrose and not fat that is the real culprit in the currently high incidence of heart disease.

Accordingly most nutritional information these days is about fat, fibre, and energy and it would be easy to forget that you should also eat plenty of vitamins and minerals. If any of these are in short supply your health will suffer and at the very least you will be tired and have no enthusiasm for life.

Vitamin vitality

Towards the end of the last century research showed that animals could not live on adequate supplies of proteins, fats and carbohydrates alone. Minute quantities of other substances were required for proper health and growth.

In the early days of nutrition research a vitamin was recognized by its absence. Vitamin B deficiency was found to cause beriberi and vitamin D deficiency caused rickets. However, increased research has given us much more idea of how vitamins actually work. For example, the function of vitamin B_1 in the cells of the body is to act as an enzyme in the oxidation of foodstuffs to provide energy. The depth of knowledge about each vitamin varies considerably and many of them seem to perform more than one function.

Here is a summary of some of the known functions of the most important vitamins. It also lists major and minor sources of the vitamins and indicates whether they are sensitive to air, light, heat or water.

Vitamins: Summary Chart

Vitamins	Functions	Sources	Others	Loss
A	Maintenance of healthy growth. Concerned with healthy vision and the ability to adapt to poor light. Maintenance of healthy conditions in the respiratory tract.	carrots butter spinach margarine cheese	cream eggs milk	air
B$_1$ (Thiamine)	Maintenance of healthy growth. Aids digestion. Maintenance of healthy nervous system. May be involved in maintenance of a healthy heart.	wheatgerm Brazil nuts peanuts	oatmeal wholemeal bread yeast vegetables nuts	heat water
B$_2$ (Riboflavin)	Maintenance of healthy growth. Aids conversion of nutrients in the diet into energy. Concerned with healthy vision.		Cheddar cheese eggs milk broccoli wholegrain cereals leafy vegetables bananas	water light
Niacin (**B**$_3$)	Aids conversion of nutrients in food to energy. Improves circulation and helps maintain proper brain activity.	instant coffee peanuts	nuts cheese eggs yeast dried fruit pulses watercress	water
Pantothenate (**B**$_5$)	Important for increasing resistance to infection. Important in the proper	Brewer's yeast yeast extract	yogurt eggs milk	water heat light

Vitamins	Functions	Sources	Others	Loss
	functioning of the respiratory system.		cheese cereal nuts green vegetables	
B_6	Aids conversion of nutrients in food to energy. Maintenance of healthy nervous system. Important in resistance to infection.		Brewer's yeast wheatgerm molasses milk eggs avocado pears	water
B_{12}	Important in strengthening the immune system and in mental health. Promotes the growth of healthy blood cells. Relieves muscle fatigue and increases energy.		eggs cheese soya beans beansprouts peanuts bananas	water
Folic Acid	Works with vitamin B_{12} in the formation of red blood cells. Essential for the correct metabolism of RNA and DNA. Strengthens the body's immune system.	spinach watercress	walnuts carrots wholewheat soya apricot melon Brewer's yeast	water light heat air
C	Essential for healthy growth of cells and connective tissue. Helps to increase resistance to infection.	blackcurrants rosehip watercress green peppers broccoli citrus fruits beansprouts new potatoes	all fruit and vegetables	air water

Vitamins	Functions	Sources	Others	Loss
D	Essential to healthy bone and teeth formation.	sunshine margarine	eggs butter cheese	light air
E	Acts as a natural anti-oxidant for fatty acids and proteins as well as certain vitamins in the body.	peanut butter safflower oil soyabean oil	wheatgerm eggs green vegetables	air

Minerals, too, play a part in the functioning of the enzyme systems in the cells and they also form part of the structure of the body. Calcium and phosphate form the skeleton and iron is an ingredient in the blood. Other minerals like magnesium, manganese, copper, zinc, chloride, sulphates and many other trace elements are also needed.

Some nutritionists glibly state that the Western diet is so varied that there is no need to worry about vitamin or mineral deficiencies. Others agree that there may be problems with certain ones, such as iron and folic acid or vitamin B_6. There are some who go very much further and state that current recommended daily intake levels are far too low and that an increased intake would be beneficial to all aspects of our lives, from physical energy to mental activity. If this is the case then even more care needs to be taken with our food choices than that indicated in the general guidelines.

The working of vitamins and minerals is still not fully understood, but we do know that they may need to be taken in the correct proportion with each other. The B complex vitamins, for example, seem to act far better together than they do in isolation, i.e., vitamin B_6 is important for the absorption of vitamin B_{12}. Another example is the relationship between vitamins A and E. The latter seems to protect against loss of effectiveness in the former and vitamin D is very important in the bone building process along with calcium and phosphate.

Making the most of vitamins and minerals

These kinds of relationships mean that it may well be worth a bit of extra planning to ensure that the complementary vitamins are taken together in the diet. This really need not be at all difficult. In the case of vitamins A and E all that would be required is a combination of bread and cheese or spinach salad with safflower oil or a peanut butter sauce on your carrots.

A vegetarian diet does not lose anything nutritionally by leaving out meat or fish. Dairy produce provides many of the vitamins which meat eaters usually gain from animal sources and fruit and vegetables are the major sources of most of the others. Vegans may have to watch their diets a little more carefully and both vegetarians and vegans need to watch their intake of iron. The problem is that vegetable sources of iron tend not to be so readily available to our bodies as iron from animal sources. Eating food rich in vitamin C helps to offset this problem, so good combinations include toast and orange juice, green peppers and watercress salad, tabbouleh with a high parsley content and lemon juice and new potatoes in their skins with scrambled eggs.

Though certain foods are rich in particular vitamins almost all food contains small amounts of at least some vitamins. To make the most of any vitamin source the food must be eaten when it is as fresh as possible. Vitamins in food do not just remain the same. Like the food itself they change over time. They can also be adversely affected by cooking and storage treatments. Some vitamins like A, C, D and E are gradually lost to the air. Vitamin C, particularly, starts to disappear from green vegetables the moment they are picked, so the quicker they get to your table the better. This means the home-grown produce picked immediately before use is freshest but frozen produce can almost match it, whereas the fresh peas or broccoli from the supermarket may be 24 hours old or more before you even see them. Other vitamins like B_2 and B_5 are light sensitive. Cooking brings its own problems. Vitamins like B_1, B_5 and E are heat sensitive and most of the B vitamins and vitamin C will leak out into the water. Folic acid is particularly sensitive to any kind of treatment at all.

Cooking to conserve vitamins

If you do want to cook some of your food, and most of us do if only to counteract the cold winter weather, then it helps to keep the cooking time to a minimum. Grilling is a fairly fast method but the ideal method is stir-frying. It is fast and efficient and everything including water-soluble vitamins are kept in the pan and served with the food. Cooking times can be kept to the absolute minimum. However, food which is stir-fried badly can be very fatty. The secret is to use as little oil as possible — maybe only one tablespoonful — in a non-stick wok or frying pan and to get the temperature pretty high before you start. It is actually possible to dispense with the oil altogether and to stir-fry in a small amount of hot vegetable stock. To my mind this is carrying things a bit far as the fat helps to bring out the flavour of the food and you do need to eat some fat in the diet.

Steaming is a useful method of keeping vitamins away from the cooking liquor. Use a steam basket in a saucepan or an electric steamer. The method is not perfect and it is still worth keeping the water in the base of the pan for soups. Anything which steams well will also cook well in the microwave for the effect is the same. A microwave can be very useful for cooking vegetables and for anything you might cook 'au bain marie' such as mousses and terrines.

Processed food

Food processing usually means that the food concerned is likely to have lost some of its essential nutrients. This is certainly true for anything that has been heat treated, so check out foods like yogurt, honey and vegetable oils. Margarine is something of an exception as the nutrients are added into the recipe in such a way that they are still there in some quantity at the end. However, margarine can hardly be described as a natural product. The choice is yours!

Any kind of refining process is also likely to lead to loss of vitamins and this is certainly true for wheat, rice and other cereals and for sugar. Accordingly the recipes in this book mainly use wholemeal flour, brown rice and dark sugars.

Energy from starch

You don't have to be very old to remember when eating lots of starchy foods was considered to be a recipe for getting fat. Today we are being encouraged to eat more cereals. It was the butter which we spread on our bread or the fatty sauce that went with our pasta or rice which caused the problems, we are told.

It has been known for a long time that starchy foods provided energy, but in the past it was always assumed that if really large amounts of energy were going to be needed, by top athletes or marathon runners for example, the best fuel would be proteins. Indeed some runners still stick to the steak-for-strength philosophy. Others report favourable results from storing up energy producing substances in the body, by eating large quantities of starch foods a day or two prior to the race.

Even the most active of us are unlikely to need this kind of 'carbohydrate loading', but it does show that these foods offer long lasting energy and most of us need to feel that our energy levels will last us through the day. So, unless you lead a sedentary life, it is important to eat more wholemeal bread, pasta, cereals, brown rice, dried pulses and starchy root vegetables like potatoes and yams. A point to remember here is that people eating a carbohydrate-rich diet may need more vitamin B_1.

Fibre facts

Implementing the suggestions for increased cereals in the diet will automatically help to increase the amount of fibre. Fibre is contained in the cell wall of plants. The greatest concentrations of fibre are generally obtained from the external surfaces of food, for example apple peel, potato skins, and the outer layers of rice and cereals. Like vitamins, the fibre values of food are often reduced by cooking, processing or refining.

Fibre in the diet is thought to play an important role in both the prevention and cure of diseases of the digestive tract, heart disease and varicose veins. There are two kinds of fibre: soluble and insoluble. Most fibre-containing foods supply a combination of the two but the proportion may vary.

Insoluble fibre assists the passage of foods through the body. It takes up water and acts as a bulking agent in the stomach. Insoluble fibre also increases the rate at which food passes through the body and at the same time it removes any toxic substances, thus helping to prevent diseases of the bowel. Soluble fibre, on the other hand, is partially broken down during digestion. It is thought to have a metabolic effect in reducing levels of cholesterol in the blood. It also delays the uptake of sugar into the blood allowing a moderate uptake over an extended period of time. It can therefore be of particular use to diabetics. Without soluble fibre the consequence of a sugar-rich meal or snack is a sudden large rise in blood sugar followed by an equally, if not more, drastic drop a short while later. Another important function of soluble fibre is that it has been shown to bind with cholesterol from food and assist in its elimination from the body. Soluble fibre is present in most fruit and vegetables, in pulses and in many grains, but especially in oats. Kidneys beans and sweet corn are particularly rich in soluble fibre.

The high vitality way

All the known facts about food lead to the conclusion that a careful selection of really fresh food is the best way to health and vitality. All the essential nutrients will be present and you will be sure of providing your body with the kind of food it really needs to work at maximum effectiveness. So the answer lies in eating at least one raw food meal a day, coupled with quick cooking methods and an awareness of how to conserve vitamins, minerals and fibre.

Food is also meant to be enjoyed and there is no need for a healthy way of eating to result in boring or unappetizing food. You don't have to crunch through mountains of shredded cabbage or force down dry and tasteless grains to enjoy a high vitality diet. Plenty of fresh fruit and salads can be complemented with the kind of recipes found in Chapter 2. These use mainly raw untreated ingredients and there is no cooking at all. Many of the recipes also make good starters and desserts for meals where the main course is cooked.

Other chapters use quick-cooking methods or show how cereals and other starchy foods can be made into really interesting dishes. The last chapter includes some dishes which may take rather longer to cook or use a little more fat and sugar than you might want to use every day. These are for entertaining and for high days and holidays.

1
STARTING UP

Breakfast at the double

Breakfast in a glass

There are all sorts of healthy breakfasts in a glass that have been advocated by both experts and enthusiasts. Here are just a few to try. Each is enough for one glass.

¼ pint (140ml) fresh skimmed milk
juice of 1 orange, freshly squeezed

1. Simply mix and drink.

5 oz (140g) natural yogurt
3 oz (85g) fresh blackcurrants or
   raspberries
or
1 mango, 2 kiwi fruit or 1 pear
skimmed milk, to taste

1. Place all the ingredients in a blender and process until smooth. Add a little milk if the mixture is too thick.

1 banana
1 tablespoon wheatgerm
¼ pint (140ml) fresh skimmed milk

1. Mash the banana with a fork and mix with the wheatgerm and then the milk. Stir and drink at once.

Oat porridge

Traditional:

6 oz (170g) medium oatmeal
2 pints (1.1 litres) water

1. Soak the oatmeal overnight in the water.
2. Next morning bring the water to the boil. Turn down the heat and cook slowly for 20–25 minutes until it is thick.
3. Serve with skimmed milk and your choice of topping.

Quick:

8 oz (225g) rolled oats or porridge oats
2 pints (1.1 litres) water

1. Place the oats and water in a pan and bring to the boil.
2. Stir and then lower the heat and simmer for 5 minutes, stirring occasionally.
3. Serve with skimmed milk and your choice of topping.

Oats are high in fibre and a good source of folic acid. Serve with a glass of orange juice to increase the iron absorption.

Toppings:
Maple syrup
Fresh summer berries
Raisins and chopped nuts
Chopped dates

Finnish fruit porridge

This recipe is popular all over Finland. It may be served warm or cold. It can also be made with oats or rye. You can usually get more juice out of the fruit if you heat it in a saucepan first until fairly hot and then rub through a sieve. However, more vitamin C is likely to be lost this way.

½ lb (225g) blackcurrants, bilberries or
    blueberries
½ pint (285ml) skimmed milk
water
2 oz (55g) wholemeal semolina
light muscovado sugar or honey, to taste

1. Rub the fruit through a sieve and measure the resulting purée. Subtract this amount from 1 pint (570ml). The result will be somewhere around ¾ pint (425ml).
2. Make up the milk to this amount with water and bring to the boil. Sprinkle in the semolina and cook for 10–15 minutes or until the semolina is cooked, stirring all the time.
3. Remove from the heat and whisk in the fruit purée. Continue whisking until the mixture is light and frothy.
4. Serve with a sprinkling of sugar or honey if desired.

Apple muesli

Muesli was originally developed by Dr Bircher-Benner at his clinic in Switzerland. The emphasis was on the raw fruit content rather than the cereal. Today there is a wide range of different mixes and any of them can be used as a base. Ring the changes through the year by using soft fruits like raspberries, blackcurrants and peaches when they are in season.

4 level tablespoons rolled oats
12 tablespoons water
4 tablespoons lemon juice
4 large crisp eating apples
2 tablespoons raisins
2 tablespoons grated nuts (hazelnuts, almonds or walnuts)

1. Place the oats in a large bowl and spoon on the water. Leave to stand overnight.
2. Stir in the lemon juice. Grate the apples, cores and all into the mixture, stirring to prevent discoloration after each one.
3. Stir in the raisins and nuts and serve at once.

Crunchy muesli with yogurt

Choose a crunchy toasted muesli base with as little added sugar as possible. Mangoes, plums, apricots or pears all work well as a topping.

4 tablespoons crunchy muesli base
4 oz (115g) mixed dried fruit, chopped
(apricots, bananas, prunes and raisins)
2 tablespoons roughly chopped nuts
1 green-skinned apple, chopped
8 oz (225g) plain live yogurt

1. Mix the crunchy muesli base with the chopped fruit and nuts in a large bowl.
2. Spoon into individual bowls and top with a good dollop of yogurt.
3. Decorate with a little chopped fruit in season.

High fibre recipe: choose bananas for their good mix of B complex vitamins including folic acid and traces of vitamin B_{12}.

Yogurt

It is worth checking that the yogurt you are buying is live yogurt. A rough rule of thumb is that set yogurt is live, and stirred or runny yogurt is not.

Check the 'consume by' date on your yogurt. This is the date to which significant numbers in the culture remain alive and active. Store in the fridge.

You may like to look out for a new type of yogurt called *BA Live* which contains two extra cultures which work together to maintain a healthy balance in the intestine and so aid digestion.

Winter fruit bowl

Three or four sliced kumquats give an extra tangy flavour to this dish. Add while the dried fruit is still warm for the best flavour. It is quite a good idea to cook larger quantities of dried fruit and store in the fridge. All kinds of fresh fruit in season can be added to the mix with the orange juice.

1¼ pints (710ml) water
6 oz (170g) no-soak dried apricots or mixed fruits
2 oz (55g) raisins
1 stick cinnamon
2 whole cloves
2 Conference pears, peeled and cored
2 clementines or seedless satsumas, segmented
¼ pint (140ml) orange juice
a little grated orange rind

1. Bring the water to the boil and add the dried fruit and spices. Cover and simmer for 10–15 minutes until the fruit is tender. Remove from the heat.
2. Cut the pears into chunks and add to the hot fruit with the raisins. Leave to stand until cold. Just before serving add the clementine segments, orange juice and rind.

Black fruit salad with wheatgerm

4 oz (115g) black cherries
4 oz (115g) black grapes, halved and seeded
4 oz (115g) blackcurrants, blueberries or bilberries
juice of 1 lemon
5 oz (140g) carton natural yogurt
4 tablespoons wheatgerm
raw-cane sugar, to taste
sprigs of mint or chervil, to garnish

1. Mix all the fruits together with the lemon juice and spoon into four individual bowls.
2. Top with a dollop of yogurt sprinkled with wheatgerm over the top and sugar if desired. Garnish with fresh herbs.

This recipe gives a good combination of vitamins A (yogurt) and E (wheatgerm).

Manhattan melon bowl

Vary the supporting fruit to fit the season – apricots, tangerine segments, blackcurrants, apples, bananas and mangoes can all be pressed into service.

2 small ogen melons, cut in half and
  seeded
2 ripe pears
juice of 2 lemons
12–16 strawberries
2 kiwi fruit, peeled and sliced
juice of 2 oranges
a handful of fresh mint

1. Cut balls from the melons with a melon baller. Tidy the melon skins with a teaspoon and keep on one side.
2. Core and dice the pears and mix with the lemon juice to prevent discoloration. Add the melon balls and all the remaining ingredients and toss well together. Spoon back into the melon skins and serve at once.

Sunshine muffins

This simple breakfast dish can be varied by adding a layer of creamed sweetcorn or spinach to the muffins before adding the egg.

4 wholemeal muffins
butter or polyunsaturated firm margarine
4 eggs
1 tablespoon vinegar

1. Split and toast the muffins. Butter or spread with margarine.
2. Poach the eggs in boiling water mixed with a little vinegar.
3. Place one egg on a half muffin and serve with the remaining half.

Indian toast

Any kind of cheese firm enough to grate can be used in this recipe. If using goat's cheese leave out the curry powder and use plain chutney, otherwise the flavours will not mix too happily.

4 oz (115g) firm cheese, grated
2 tablespoons ginger chutney
½ teaspoon mild curry powder
4 large slices wholemeal bread
4 tomatoes, sliced

1. Mix the cheese, chutney and curry powder to a thick paste.
2. Toast the bread on each side and top each slice with tomato slices.
3. Spread the cheese mixture over the top and bake under a hot grill for 3–4 minutes until the cheese is bubbly.

When there is time to spare

Smoked tofu kedgeree _____

2 oz (55g) butter or firm margarine
12 oz (340g) cooked long grain brown rice
12 oz (340g) smoked tofu, cubed
3 eggs, hard boiled and chopped
pinch curry powder
sea salt and freshly ground black pepper
4 fl oz (115ml) soured cream or Greek
  yogurt
4 tablespoons freshly chopped parsley

This recipe offers a very rich protein dish with a good carbohydrate and vitamin content. Serve with tomatoes to boost the vitamin C content. A good way to start the day if you are very active, or serve as a brunch dish.

1. Heat the butter in a deep saucepan and toss the rice in this until thoroughly coated.
2. Add the tofu and eggs and fold carefully into the rice.
3. Mix the remaining ingredients in a cup and pour over the kedgeree.
4. Carefully toss over the heat to warm through and serve at once.

Soya crêpes

Soya flour produces a really light and fluffy pancake which is more like a drop scone than a French crêpe. For more body use half soya flour and half wholemeal flour.

3 oz (85g) soya flour
7 fl oz (200ml) soya milk or skimmed dairy milk
2 eggs, separated
sea salt
sunflower seed oil

The iron in soya beans and soya products is more easily absorbed than iron from other vegetable sources.

1. Carefully mix the soya flour with a little of the milk to form a smooth paste. Gradually add the rest of the milk, beating well to prevent any lumps forming.
2. Add the egg yolks and salt. Whisk the egg whites until really stiff. Add one tablespoonful to the batter, then fold in the rest.
3. Heat a very little cooking oil in a heavy-based pan. Drop large spoonfuls of the batter onto the hot pan and cook for a minute or so until brown on one side.
4. Turn over and cook the second side. Serve at once.

Serving suggestion:

Serve topped with fresh fruit and yogurt, maple syrup or honey when you want to boost the protein content of your breakfast.

Grilled polenta with tomato and cheese

This is an anglicized version of an Italian favourite. I like a little of my favourite pickle under the cheese for a change.

1½ pints (850ml) water
4 oz (115g) yellow cornmeal
1 teaspoon sea salt
3 oz (85g) butter or firm margarine

1. Bring the water to the boil in a saucepan and pour in the cornmeal in a slow but steady stream, stirring all the time. Add the salt and two-thirds of the butter or

2 oz (55g) Parmesan cheese, grated
¼ teaspoon grated nutmeg
4 tomatoes, thinly sliced
3 oz (85g) Cheddar cheese, grated

This recipe is gluten-free. Choose yellow rather than white cornmeal for its vitamin A content.

margarine and continue stirring until the mixture thickens.
2. Continue cooking over a low heat for 20–30 minutes, stirring fairly frequently. The mixture should be thick and smooth.
3. Add the Parmesan cheese and nutmeg and spoon into a basin. Leave to cool, then slice the polenta.
4. Melt the remaining fat and brush the polenta with this. Place under a hot grill and cook for 2 or 3 minutes.
5. Turn over and top with sliced tomatoes and cheddar cheese. Return to the grill and cook until the cheese is bubbly.

Watercress and Ricotta omelette

This only serves two. Double up the quantities for four and use a larger omelette pan or cook two.

3 tablespoons Ricotta cheese
a little minced garlic (optional)
½ bunch watercress, coarsely chopped
1 tablespoon grated Parmesan
4 eggs
4 tablespoons water
sea salt and freshly ground black pepper
sunflower or safflower oil

1. Mix the Ricotta cheese with the garlic (if using), watercress and Parmesan and keep on one side.
2. Beat the eggs with the water and seasoning and pour into a pre-heated and lightly-oiled omelette pan.
3. Gently stir to make a light omelette.
4. Dot with spoonfuls of the cheese and watercress mixture. Fold up and serve at once.

Pepper scramble

Take care not to overcook the peppers — they should be relatively crisp to the bite.

½ small green pepper, seeded
½ small red pepper, seeded
1 teaspoon polyunsaturated cooking oil
1 teaspoon green peppercorns (optional)
4 eggs, beaten
3 tablespoons water
sea salt and freshly ground black pepper

1. Finely dice the peppers and gently fry in the cooking oil in a non-stick pan. They will take about 2–3 minutes to soften a little.
2. Beat the peppercorns, if using, with the eggs and water and pour into the pan with the peppers.
3. Scramble for a minute or two until lightly set. Season to taste and serve at once.

Brunch rosti

This dish is rather like a cross between Swiss rosti which does not use egg and Spanish tortilla which uses rather more. Serve with grilled tomatoes and creamed spinach or with stuffed mushrooms (see page 69).

3 large potatoes, peeled
1 large onion, peeled and chopped finely
3 eggs, beaten
1 tablespoon plain wholemeal flour
1 tablespoon cooking oil

Variations:

Add fresh herbs or spices like cumin or celery salt and paprika for a change of flavour.

Served as suggested, this recipe offers a good mix of all the major vitamins.

1. Grate the potatoes into a bowl and quickly mix with the chopped onions, egg and flour.
2. Heat the oil in a heavy-based frying pan and spoon in the potato mixture. Reduce the heat and cook over a low to medium heat for about 10–15 minutes until the base of the rosti is crisp and golden.
3. Using a large fish slice turn over in one piece and cook on the second side for the same period of time. Cut into wedges to serve.

Baked in advance

Everyday wholemeal bread _____

My father made this recipe every week for 30 years. He liked a fairly wet dough but if it is too sticky to work with, add a little more flour.

13–14 fl oz (370–400ml) lukewarm water
½ oz (15g) dried yeast
1 lb (455g) wholemeal flour
1 teaspoon sea salt

Bread made from wholemeal flour offers a good source of B vitamins, vitamin E, potassium and magnesium. Also high fibre content.

1. Mix the water and yeast and leave to stand in a warm place for about 10 minutes until frothy.
2. Place flour and salt in a bowl and pour on the yeast and water. Mix together with your hands and knead in the bowl for 7–9 minutes.
3. Place in a loaf tin and cover with oiled paper. Leave in a warm place to stand until double in size. This takes about 1 hour.
4. Set the oven to 230°C/450°F (Gas Mark 8). Bake for 35 minutes until cooked. To see if the loaf is cooked, remove from the tin and rap the base with your knuckles. It should sound hollow. If it doesn't cook a little longer.
5. Leave on a wire rack to cool.

Bread rolls

1½ lb (680g) plain wholemeal flour
1 teaspoon salt
1 sachet easy bake yeast
1 oz (30g) margarine
pinch raw-cane sugar
19–20 fl oz (540–570ml) lukewarm water
1 egg white, beaten
poppy seeds or sesame seeds

1. Place the flour, salt and yeast in a bowl and mix well. Cut the margarine into small pieces and rub into the dry ingredients.
2. Add a pinch of sugar. Mix in the water to make a good dough.
3. Turn onto a floured surface and knead for 10 minutes until it is no longer sticky.
4. Shape into knots and crescents with tapering ends. Brush with egg white and sprinkle with poppy seeds or with sesame seeds. Slash some crescents along the top.
5. Place on a greased baking tray and leave in a warm place until double in size.
6. Bake at 230°C/450°F (Gas Mark 8) for 10–15 minutes until cooked. Tap the base — if it sounds hollow, they are cooked.
7. Cool on a wire rack.

Norwegian soda bread

8 oz (225g) rye flour
8 oz (225g) wholemeal flour
1 teaspoon baking powder
1½ teaspoons bicarbonate of soda
1 teaspoon sea salt
1 tablespoon light muscovado sugar
8 fl oz (240ml) buttermilk
1 egg, lightly beaten
1 fl oz (30ml) sunflower seed oil or melted
   butter

*The use of rye flour does not result in a
particularly dark coloured loaf. The reason
why so many commercial rye and wheat
loaves are so dark in colour is that they
have been coloured with caramel. If you
prefer a darker loaf, substitute a dark brown
molasses sugar for the light muscovado.*

1. Set the oven to 220°C/425°F
   (Gas Mark 7) and grease a large baking
   sheet.
2. Mix the rye and wholemeal flour in a
   bowl and stir in the baking power,
   bicarbonate of soda, salt and sugar.
3. Make a well in the centre and stir in the
   buttermilk, egg and fat. Mix to a smooth
   dough.
4. Transfer the dough to a floured surface
   and knead lightly. Divide into two equal
   parts and shape each one into a flat
   round shape about ½-inch (1cm) thick.
5. Place on the baking tray and bake for
   20–25 minutes or until lightly browned.
   Transfer to a wire rack and serve warm
   or cold.

Black rye bread

This is an adaptation of an old Victorian recipe. It has a very robust and definite flavour and is excellent served with a good strong cheese.

I have used activated dried yeast in the recipe as it is extremely useful for reducing the time required to make bread. The yeast can be added just as it is and the dough does not need to be kneaded more than once.

12 oz (340g) rye flour
7 oz (200g) wholemeal flour
1½ teaspoons salt
1 × ½ oz (15g) sachet activated dried yeast
1 teaspoon ground coriander
1 teaspoon ground cinnamon
½ pint (300ml) lukewarm water
3 tablespoons black treacle or molasses
2 tablespoons clear honey
2 oz (55g) melted butter

Good source of B vitamins, vitamin E and fibre.

1. Place the flours, salt, yeast and spices in a large bowl. Make a well in the centre.
2. Mix the water, treacle or molasses, honey and melted butter and pour into the well in the flour. Mix to a stiff dough. If the dough is too stiff add a little more water.
3. Turn out onto a floured board and knead for 10 minutes. Shape into a large ball and flatten slightly.
4. Place on a greased baking tray and cover with a polythene bag. Leave to rise for 1–1½ hours until the dough has doubled in size.
5. Preheat the oven to 220°C/425°F (Gas Mark 7) Lightly brush the top of the loaf with a little cooking oil and bake for 35–40 minutes.
6. Test the underside of the bread with your knuckles. If it sounds hollow it is cooked. If not, reduce the heat to 190°C/375°F (Gas Mark 5) and continue cooking for a further 5–10 minutes. Leave to cool on a wire rack.

American carrot muffins

These deliciously light muffins are best eaten warm. Reheat in a hot oven. American muffins are rather like large fluffy buns. They are popular at breakfast and brunch when they are eaten instead of bread.

6 oz (170g) wholemeal flour
3 oz (85g) white flour
1 tablespoon baking powder
½ teaspoon ground cinnamon
¼ teaspoon salt
2 large eggs (size 1)
3 oz (85g) dark muscovado sugar
6 fl oz (170ml) milk
2 fl oz (60 ml) sunflower seed oil
4 oz (115g) carrots, coarsely grated
3 oz (85g) raisins
2 oz (55g) chopped walnuts

1. Set the oven to 190°C/375°F (Gas Mark 5) and grease a tray of muffin pans.
2. Mix the flours, baking powder, cinnamon and salt together.
3. Whisk the eggs and sugar in a large bowl. Then whisk in the milk and oil. Stir in the remaining ingredients.
4. Pour over the dry ingredients and fold all together. Spoon into the muffin pans.
5. Bake for 25 minutes. Turn out onto a rack to cool.

Apple sunflower muffins

Makes 12

These muffins are excellent instead of cake at tea time. Eat them whilst still warm or leave to cool on a wire rack and reheat just before eating.

8 oz (225g) wholemeal flour
2 tablespoons sunflower seeds
1½ teaspoons baking powder
½ teaspoon salt
½ teaspoon ground cinnamon
1 egg, well beaten
9 fl oz (250ml) milk
1 apple, coarsely grated
2 tablespoons raisins

1. Mix together the first five dry ingredients.
2. Mix in the egg and milk and add to a bowl with the apple and raisins.
3. Spoon into lightly-greased muffin tins. Bake at 200°C/400°F (Gas Mark 6) for 15–20 minutes until risen and firm.

Blackcurrant muffins

The original recipe for these muffins came from a friend in Massachusetts who used fresh blueberries and these and English bilberries can be used when in season. Frozen fruit should be avoided as it makes the mixture too wet.

Eat these American-style muffins for breakfast or tea. They are best served lightly heated.

4 oz (115g) butter
3 oz (85g) raw cane sugar
2 large eggs (size 1)
3 oz (85g) fresh blackcurrants, mashed
12 oz (340g) wholemeal flour
2 teaspoons baking powder
½ teaspoon salt
4 fl oz (115ml) milk
12 oz (340g) fresh whole blackcurrants
grated nutmeg, to taste

1. Set the oven to 190°C/375°F (Gas Mark 5) and grease a tray of muffin pans.
2. Beat the butter and almost all the sugar until creamy and then beat in the eggs one at a time.
3. Next add together the mashed blackcurrants. Sift the flour, baking powder and salt together and add half to the butter and eggs.
4. Next add half the milk and then the remaining flour and milk. Fold in the remaining fruit.
5. Spoon the batter into the muffin pans. Sprinkle with the remaining sugar mixed with nutmeg if liked.
6. Bake for 30–35 minutes until golden brown. Leave to cool in the muffin pans.

Blackcurrants

Blackcurrants are one of the richest fruit sources of vitamin C. A 3½ oz (100g) portion of stewed blackcurrants contains an average of five times the recommended intake of vitamin C — so the raw fruit is likely to contain even more.

2
FRESH ON THE TABLE

Cocktails, soups and savoury sorbets

Iced vegetable cocktail

Use small sticks of celery from near the centre of the head. Outside sticks will be too stringy for this recipe.

1 lb (455g) tomatoes, peeled and seeded
1 carrot, finely grated
2 small sticks celery, chopped
2 tablespoons freshly chopped parsley
2 teaspoons freshly chopped mint
8 fl oz (240ml) vegetable stock
½ teaspoon yeast extract
a few drops Tabasco sauce
juice and grated rind of 1 orange or 1
    lemon

Garnish:

sprigs of mint
lemon or orange slices

1. Place all the ingredients except the garnishes in a food processor or blender and process until smooth.
2. Chill for 1 hour before serving with sprigs of mint and lemon or orange slices.

Good fresh source of vitamin B complex and C with some vitamin A.

Tomato and herb sorbet

The alcohol content of this recipe is fairly high and it is this that stops the sorbet from freezing so hard that it is impossible to eat. If you want to reduce the alcohol content, replace some of the vodka with more tomato juice and remove from the freezer 20–30 minutes before serving. If you remove the vodka altogether you may have to crush the frozen sorbet with a rolling pin!

1 lb (455g) tomatoes, peeled and seeded
¼ pint (140ml) tomato juice
2 tablespoons light muscovado sugar
2 fl oz (60ml) Vodka or Aquavit
2 tablespoons freshly chopped herbs, e.g.,
    basil, parsley, oregano or tarragon
1 teaspoon lemon juice
a few drops of Tabasco sauce
1 egg white, stiffly beaten

1. Blend the tomatoes in a food processor or a blender or rub them through a sieve. Mix with all the remaining ingredients except the egg white and place in the freezer.
2. After about 1¾ hours, when the mixture begins to freeze round the edges, beat well and then fold in the egg white.
3. Return to the freezer and beat after 1 hour and then after another hour or place in a sorbetière and freeze. The sorbet will be ready to eat in about 3 hours.

Curried cucumber sherbet

This sherbet has an unusual grainy texture and a very refreshing and exotic flavour. If it has been in the freezer overnight you will need to thaw it for 20–30 minutes before serving. Do not store for more than a few days or the taste will be rather bitter.

4-inch (10cm) piece cucumber, chopped
3 tablespoons Greek yogurt
1 teaspoon lemon juice
1 teaspoon freshly grated root ginger
½ teaspoon mild curry powder
1 tablespoon light muscovado sugar
1 egg white, stiffly whisked

1. Blend the cucumber in a food processor or blender with all the other ingredients except the egg white.
2. Spoon into a container and place in the freezer. After 2 hours, when the mixture begins to freeze round the edges, beat with a fork and fold in the beaten egg white.
3. Return to the freezer to set, beating after 1 and then 2 hours or transfer to a sorbetière and freeze. The sherbet is ready to eat after 3 hours.

Fresh plum soup

It is very important to choose really ripe plums for this mid-European inspired soup. If the plums are not very ripe the result will be both sour and lumpy.

1 lb (455g) plums, stoned and halved
2 oz (55g) ground almonds
1 teaspoon ground cinnamon
4 spring onions, finely chopped
¾ pint (425ml) vegetable stock
2 tablespoons dry white wine or sherry

1. Place the plums in a blender or food processor with the almonds, cinnamon, onions, and a little of the stock. Blend until smooth.
2. Stir in the rest of the stock and leave to stand in the fridge for 4 hours. Just before serving add wine or sherry.

Chilled avocado soup

2 ripe avocados, peeled, stoned and chopped
juice of 1 lemon
5 oz (140g) natural yogurt
1 pint (570ml) vegetable stock, chilled
sea salt and freshly ground black pepper

1. Mash, sieve or blend the avocados with the lemon juice and yogurt.
2. Stir in the vegetable stock and seasoning and beat well together.
3. Garnish with chopped chives and serve at once.

Garnish:

2 tablespoons chopped chives

Avocados have a high fat content for a vegetable, but it is mostly monounsaturated fat. Avocados are also a good source of vitamin B$_6$.

Tomato and cucumber soup

If you don't want to use commercially produced tomato juice you can make your own by puréeing peeled and seeded tomatoes. But unless really, really ripe and flavoursome tomatoes are used the juice may well taste insipid and need the attention of some concentrated tomato purée.

1¾ pints (1 litre) tomato juice
juice and grated rind of 2 large oranges
10 oz (280g) natural yogurt
½ cucumber, grated
1 tablespoon freshly chopped parsley
sea salt and freshly ground black pepper

1. Pour the tomato juice into a large bowl and whisk in the orange rind and juice and the yogurt.
2. When the mixture is well blended chill for 1 hour.
3. Stir in the cucumber, parsley and season to taste. Serve at once.

Melon and orange soup

1 large ripe honeydew melon
½ teaspoon grated orange rind
juice of 1 orange

Garnish:

4 slices fresh lemon
sprigs of mint or chervil

Good source of potassium with some vitamin C. If you use more expensive yellow ogen and cantaloupe melons in place of honeydew, the vitamin A content leaps up.

1. Halve the melon and remove the seeds. Scoop out the flesh with a spoon and place in a blender or food processor with the remaining ingredients except the garnishes. Blend until smooth and chill.
2. To serve, spoon into bowl and float a slice of lemon on the top and garnish with a sprig of chervil.

Gazpacho

This lovely fresh and summery soup comes from the sunshine of Andalucia. There the tomatoes are so ripe and full of flavour they do not need any help. Unfortunately English and Dutch tomatoes rarely taste like this and tomato purée helps to pep them up a bit. Using red peppers only helps to improve the colour of the soup but any colour can be used. Large onions will give a much stronger onion flavour than most spring onions so reduce the quantity by a third to a half if you have to use these.

2 lb (900g) very ripe tomatoes, skinned, seeded and chopped
1 red pepper, seeded and chopped
3-inch (7.5cm) piece cucumber, diced
2 tablespoons finely chopped spring onion
1 teaspoon freshly chopped garlic
5 tablespoons cider or wine vinegar
4 tablespoons extra virgin olive oil
1½ tablespoons tomato purée
6–8 fl oz (170–240ml) water

Garnishes:

½ red pepper, seeded and diced
½ green pepper, seeded and diced
2-inch (5cm) piece cucumber diced

1. Place the chopped tomatoes, red pepper, cucumber, spring onion and garlic in a blender or food processor with the vinegar. Blend until smooth.
2. Stir in the remaining ingredients except the garnishes and chill for 1 hour.
3. Prepare the garnishes just before serving and serve in separate bowls.

Green peppers

Green peppers are among the richest vegetable sources of vitamin C. Broccoli tops are their only rival. Weight for weight these vegetables can provide twice as much vitamin C as citrus fruits but they must be fresh and uncooked.

Yogurt soup with spring onion and ginger

½ pint (285ml) well-flavoured vegetable
  stock (see below)
1½ lb (680g) plain yogurt
1 tablespoon lemon juice
2-inch (5cm) piece cucumber, grated
8 spring onions, finely chopped
1 teaspoon freshly grated root ginger
freshly ground black pepper

Vegetable stock:

2 carrots
2 onions
1 courgette
2 pints (1.1 litres) water
onion skins (optional)

Garnish:

spring onions

1. Mix the stock you have made in advance
   (for method see below) and yogurt in a
   large bowl. Stir in the remaining
   ingredients and chill for 1 hour.

Vegetable stock:

1. Boil the carrots, onions and courgette in
   the water for 40 minutes. Add some
   onion skins to the water if you require a
   good colour. The liquid should then be
   reduced by half.
2. Drain the vegetables very well by
   pressing through a fine mesh sieve.
   (If you need a well-flavoured stock in a
   hurry, you could add a little yeast extract
   to liquid left from steaming vegetables.
   Take care not to overdo the extract as it
   can taste quite strong.)

Garnish:

1. Slice down the length of the spring
   onions, almost to the base.
2. Place in a bowl of cold water until they
   have opened out and curled.

Starters and specialities

Watercress pâté

For greatest freshness serve at once. However, a better texture and flavour is obtained by chilling for 1 hour before serving.

1 bunch watercress
4 oz (115g) goat's cheese
5 spring onions, finely chopped
3 tablespoons quark or fromage frais
freshly ground black pepper

Vegan version:

1 bunch watercress
8 oz (225g) silken tofu
3 oz (85g) ground almonds
6 spring onions, finely chopped
2 tablespoons freshly chopped parsley
a little grated lemon rind
sea salt and freshly ground black pepper

1. Place all the ingredients for whichever version you have chosen to make in a bowl and mix well with a fork.
2. Spoon into a pâté dish.

Serving suggestions:

Serve as a starter to the main meal of the day, or in sandwiches or on canapés.

Watercress

Watercress is a good source of folic acid. To get the most out of watercress you should eat it little and often. The fresher it is the better it will be for you. Folic acid, particularly, is susceptible to air and light.

Marinated aubergines

This deliciously unusual recipe for aubergines can be served as a starter on its own or as part of a mixed hors d'oeuvre. It is also very good drained and used in sandwiches.

1 large aubergine (1 lb/455g)
sea salt
½ pint (285ml) extra virgin olive oil
3 tablespoons cider or wine vinegar
2 tablespoons dried oregano
pinch dried thyme
freshly ground black pepper
2 small dried red chillis
2 cloves garlic

Good source of monounsaturated fatty acids.

1. Cut the aubergine into thick slices ⅛-inch (0.25cm) across. Place in layers in a colander sprinkling well with salt as you go. Weight with a heavy bowl and leave to stand for 1 hour.
2. Rinse each slice under cold running water and pat dry with kitchen paper.
3. Mix together the oil, vinegar, herbs and pepper. Layer the aubergine slices in a deep dish pouring the marinade over as you go and adding the chillis and garlic here and there. Pour any remaining marinade over the top.
4. Cover and leave to stand in the fridge for 3 days, stirring once a day.

Cheese, herb and sesame log

4–5 tablespoons sesame seeds
1 lb (455g) curd cheese
4 oz (115g) farmhouse Cheddar cheese,
   grated
1 small red pepper, seeded and diced
1 small green pepper, seeded and diced
½ bunch spring onions, finely chopped
1 tablespoon each freshly chopped parsley
   and tarragon
½ teaspoon freshly chopped thyme or
   oregano
1–2 tablespoons natural yogurt

Garnish:

sprigs of parsley

1. Toast the sesame seeds under a hot grill, taking care to keep them on the move as they burn easily. Leave to cool.
2. Mix the two cheeses and then stir in all the remaining ingredients, except the garnish, adding sufficient yogurt to give a good firm but not too dry consistency.
3. Chill for 15 minutes, wrap in Bakewell paper and then roll into a log about 8 inches (20cm) long.
4. Just before serving, remove the Bakewell paper and roll in toasted sesame seeds. Cut into slices and garnish with sprigs of parsley.

Avocado with walnut dressing

For a more elegant serving, peel the avocado halves, slice, and arrange in a fan shape for each serving place. Top with the walnut dressing and garnish with pretty leaves in season.

2 large ripe avocados, stoned and halved
lemon juice, as required

Walnut dressing:

5 oz (140g) soured cream or fresh yogurt
6–8 walnut halves, chopped
3 spring onions, finely chopped
3 radishes, finely chopped
2 tablespoons freshly chopped parsley
sherry, as required.

1. Prepare the avocado and brush the exposed flesh with lemon juice to prevent discoloration.
2. Place all the dressing ingredients in a basin adding a spoonful or two of sherry to give consistency.
3. Season to taste and spoon into the avocado cavities. Serve at once.

Stilton party dip

This dip is delicious served with Sesame Pitta Bread (see page 90). Other dippers include fresh vegetable crudités like cucumber or carrot sticks, cauliflower florets, slices of pepper and small cos lettuce and chicory leaves.

3 oz (85g) butter
6 oz (170g) Stilton cheese, crumbled
3 tablespoons tawny or ruby port
2 satsumas, clementines or mandarin
  oranges
pinch cayenne pepper

1. Cream the butter and beat in the crumbled cheese and then the port.
2. Peel and segment the fruit and remove any pith or tough membranes.
3. Chop and stir into the dip with the pepper.

Dutch chicory salad

In fact, in Holland this substantial main course salad is called Endive Salad because the vegetable swaps names as it crosses the Channel! Serve with Beetroot and raisin salad (see page 55) or Kiwi salad (see page 54) and Wholemeal rolls (see page 28).

3 eggs
4 small to medium head chicory, trimmed
  and sliced
3 oz (75g) firm cheese, cubed
3 sticks celery sliced
6 radishes, sliced
a few sprigs watercress
2–3 tablespoons Whole egg mayonnaise
  (see page 49)
freshly chopped herbs to taste

This protein-rich salad makes a meal in itself. Good vitamin B complex content.

1. Hard boil the eggs and leave to cool. Shell and chop coarsely.
2. Place in a bowl with the chicory, cheese and remaining ingredients. Toss well together and serve at once.

Stuffed lettuce

You will need a large summer lettuce for this recipe. Winter glass house lettuces do not have any heart to remove! Use the centre leaves for other salads

1 large round lettuce, trimmed of old
  leaves round the outside
2 tomatoes, sliced

Filling 1:

6 eggs, beaten
4 tablespoons skimmed milk or water
½ teaspoon dried tarragon
knob of butter
6 oz (170g) cooked sweetcorn
2 oz (55g) cooked peas

Filling 2:

8 oz (225g) curd cheese
2 oz (55g) Cheddar cheese, grated
3 spring onions, finely chopped
3 oz (85g) grated celeriac
1 oz (30g) hazelnuts, chopped
sea salt and freshly ground black pepper

Garnish:

sliced kiwi fruit
sliced tomatoes
slices kumquats

1. Carefully cut out the centre heart of the lettuce. Line the cavity with the sliced tomatoes.
2. For Filling 1. mix the eggs, milk or water, tarragon and butter in a saucepan and scramble until cooked. Stir in the sweetcorn. Leave to cool.
3. Use to fill the lettuce. Top with peas. Close the lettuce leaves over the top and place in a soufflé dish. Place a plate on top and keep until required.
4. For filling 2: mix all the ingredients together in a bowl and spoon into the cavity of the lettuce and proceed as above.
5. To serve place the stuffed lettuce on a round plate and surround with the sliced fruit. Cut into wedges to serve.

These protein-rich main course dishes offer a good mix of A, B, C and D vitamins.

Cornish cheese and grapefruit salad

2 pink grapefruit, peeled and cut into segments,* kept under clingfilm until required
6–8 spring onions, trimmed and chopped
2 tablespoons freshly chopped parsley
8 tablespoons extra virgin olive oil
2 teaspoons lemon juice
freshly ground black pepper
¼ head curly endive
leaves of ½ soft round lettuce
¾ bunch watercress
6 oz (170g) Cornish Yarg (see box note) with the crusts cut off and sliced

1. Mix the spring onions and parsley with half the olive oil, the lemon juice and the pepper and keep on one side.
2. Toss the curly endive, lettuce leaves and sprigs of watercress together and arrange on four individual plates.
3. Place some slices of cheese on the centre of each salad and top with spoonfuls of the spring onion mixture.
4. Dot the grapefruit segments around the outside of the cheese and pour on the rest of the olive oil. Serve at once.

Pink grapefruit

It is the pink flesh of these grapefruits which give them their name. They are much sweeter than their ordinary counterparts and if you prefer a tart flavour you should choose the more usual variety.

Cornish Yarg

This is a mould ripened, semi-hard cheese coated in nettle leaves. It is rennet-free, being made with vegetable coagulants.

* **Segmenting grapefruit** The easiest way to produce membrane- and pith-free segments is to cut the peel off with a sharp life, cutting just below the white pith. Now cut into the fruit along the membrane lines, stopping at the centre. If you have angled the knife just right, the flesh will drop out in an attractive and easy-to-chew segment. Discard the core and cluster of membranes at the end.

Spanish orange and olive salad

Serve as an unusual and refreshing starter or as an accompaniment to a nut roast. In the latter case omit the toasted almonds.

It is important to use a good virgin olive oil for this recipe. Spanish olive oil is ideal since it is in the original recipe, and choose small black olives, as juicy as possible.

3 large oranges, peeled
juice and a little grated rind of 1 orange
4 fl oz (115ml) virgin olive oil
2 fl oz (60ml) Fino sherry
1 tablespoon freshly chopped mint
sea salt and freshly ground black pepper
3 oz (85g) small black olives
1 tablespoon raisins
1 tablespoon toasted flaked almonds
sprigs of fresh mint

1. Remove all the pith from the orange and cut into thin slices. Arrange in overlapping rings on a platter.
2. Mix the orange juice and rind with the oil, sherry, mint and seasoning and pour over the salad.
3. Sprinkle with olives, raisins and nuts. Chill for 1 hour before serving.
4. Garnish at the last minute with sprigs of mint.

Excellent source of vitamin C. Serve with a watercress salad for good iron absorption.

Olive Oil

This is high in monounsaturated fatty acids and some experts are beginning to think that these may be just as important in the prevention of heart-disease as polyunsaturated fatty acids.

Mixed leaf and nut salad

Serve as a starter

1 tablespoon pinenuts
1 tablespoon pumpkin seeds
1 tablespoon flaked almonds

1. Roast the nuts and seeds* in a dry frying pan over a medium heat. Keep them on the move to prevent them

1 tablespoon pistachio nuts
½ lollo rosso lettuce
¼ curly endive
¼ round lettuce
handful dandelion or nasturtium leaf or
corn lettuce

Dressing:

4 tablespoons walnut oil
1 teaspoon tarragon vinegar
sea salt and freshly ground black pepper

burning. Leave to cool.
2. Wash and drain the leaves very well.
   Place in a bowl.
3. Mix all the dressing ingredients and
   pour over the salad. Toss well together
   and place on four individual serving
   plates.
4. Sprinkle with the toasted nuts and serve
   at once.

* **Roasting the nuts and seeds**
Check to see if the pumpkin seeds have been removed from their skins. If not, take care when roasting as they
tend to jump out of the pan.

Roast two or three times the quantity of nuts and seeds required and you can keep what you have left over
in an airtight tin for up to a fortnight.

Mexican tomatoes

12 small tomatoes or 8 medium-sized
2 tablespoons lemon juice
2 tablespoons finely chopped onion
6-8 sprigs fresh coriander, finely chopped
2 medium-sized avocados, peeled and
   stoned
sea salt and freshly ground black pepper

Garnish:

sprigs of fresh coriander

1. Cut the tops off the tomatoes, chop and
   place in a bowl.
2. Scoop out the seeds from the centres of
   the tomatoes and discard.
3. Mix the onion and coriander with the
   tomato.
4. Rub the avocados through a sieve and
   mix in the lemon juice or blend with the
   lemon juice. Mix with the onion and
   tomato mixture and season to taste. Use
   this mixture to fill the tomatoes.
5. Garnish the tops with sprigs of fresh
   coriander and serve at once.

Salads and side salads

Carrot and herb salad

Choose the vinegar to complement the herbs chosen.

4 medium carrots, trimmed, and grated
1 small onion, peeled and very finely
  chopped
2 tablespoons freshly chopped parsley
1 teaspoon freshly chopped tarragon,
  fennel or dill
2 tablespoons virgin olive oil
2 teaspoons tarragon, plain or dill vinegar
1 teaspoon wholegrain mustard
freshly ground black pepper

1. Toss the carrots and onion in a bowl
   with the herbs.
2. Beat the oil, vinegar, mustard and
   pepper together and pour over the top.
3. Toss and serve at once.

Pazanella salad

I first had this salad as a mid-morning snack after a wine-tasting at the Villa Capezzana near
Florence in Italy.

You need plenty of basil for this recipe. Use the leaves from 10–12 sprigs. If the basil is
in short supply add a little corn lettuce or rocket. The flavour will be different but still very good.

2 oz (55g) wholemeal bread, cut into two
  thick slices
2 tablespoons water
2 teaspoons cider or wine vinegar
8 oz (225g) cherry tomatoes or 4 ordinary
  tomatoes
8 small spring onions, finely chopped
1 bunch fresh basil
2-inch (5cm) piece cucumber, diced
  (optional)
4–5 tablespoons extra virgin olive oil
Sea-salt and freshly ground black pepper

1. Place the bread in a bowl. Mix the water
   and vinegar and pour over the top.
   Leave to stand for 30 minutes.
2. Squeeze out any excess liquid from the
   bread and crumble it into another bowl.
3. Cut the cherry tomatoes into quarters or
   halves or dice the larger tomatoes. Add
   to the bowl with roughly chopped basil
   and cucumber if using.
4. Pour on the oil, season and serve at
   once.

American coleslaw
with whole egg mayonnaise

Using a whole egg rather than just the egg yolk makes a less heavy mayonnaise. However, it will not always take as much oil, so watch the mixture carefully. Flavour with mustard if liked.

These quantities will make more than enough mayonnaise so cover with clingfilm and store in the fridge to use another day.

Whole egg mayonnaise:

1 medium-sized egg
9–10 fl oz polyunsaturated salad oil
1 tablespoon white wine or cider vinegar
  or lemon juice
sea salt and freshly ground black pepper,
  to taste

Coleslaw:

¼ small head white or green cabbage,
  shredded
1 carrot, peeled and cut in thin strips with
  a cannelling knife
½ small green pepper, seeded and cut into
  thin strips

Good source of folic acid and vitamin C.
Use green cabbages for higher folic acid
content plus vitamin A.

1. Start by making the mayonnaise. Whisk the egg with a wire or electric whisk and gradually beat in the oil, pouring in a thin steady stream.
2. When all the oil has been added, fold in the vinegar or lemon juice and season to taste.
3. Mix all the coleslaw ingredients and combine with about half the whole egg mayonnaise.

Tabbouleh

This is based on a Lebanese salad that originated in the mountains and then moved down to the plains. Lebanese Tabbouleh uses a high percentage of parsley in the mix and a low percentage of bulghur. This mix is about half and half. Try experimenting to see how you like it best. You could also try mixing in some finely chopped tomato, dates or celery.

3 oz (85g) bulghur
1 large bunch parsley, chopped
4 spring onions, very finely chopped
¼ small green pepper, seeded and finely chopped
1 tablespoon freshly chopped mint
juice of 1 lemon
2 tablespoons olive oil

1. Wash the bulghur and leave to soak in 6 fl oz (170ml) water for 1 hour.
2. Drain and squeeze out all the water. Leave to stand for about 10 minutes and then squeeze again.
3. Mix with all the remaining ingredients. Chill for 30 minutes.
4. Pour off any excess liquid and serve.

Beansprout salad with Feta cheese

Serve as a main course for 2 or 3 people or as a side-salad for 4 or 5.

4 oz (115g) sprouted alfalfa
4 oz (115g) sprouted lentils or mung beans
2 oz (55g) sprouted chick peas
½ small green pepper, seeded and finely chopped
½ small onion, thinly sliced
3 tomatoes, diced
4 tablespoons olive oil
2 teaspoons wine vinegar
½ teaspoon freshly chopped thyme
6 oz (170g) Feta cheese, crumbled
8–12 black olives

1. Use the alfalfa to line a large bowl or four individual bowls.
2. Toss the sprouted beans or lentils and chick peas with the pepper, onion and tomatoes and spoon over the alfalfa.
3. Beat the olive oil with the vinegar and thyme and sprinkle over the top.
4. Add the cheese and olives and serve at once.

Sprouting

Soak the chosen beans or seeds in cold water overnight. Drain and place in a jam jar. Close the jar with a perforated lid or with a double layer of muslin held in place by a rubber band. Place on a sloping draining board so that any liquid can run out. Fill with water and empty again twice a day. The sprouts will be ready in 3–4 days. Take care to use only a spoonful or two of the dried beans or seeds for they will soon swell and grow to fill the space.

Leafy salad with croûtons and pumpkin seeds

Use any kind of flavoured vinegar that will complement the taste of the food with which you plan to serve the salad. Sherry vinegar is also worth trying for a change.

a little olive oil
1 tablespoon freshly crushed garlic
2 slices wholemeal bread
3 tablespoons pumpkin seeds
mixed salad leaves, i.e., lettuce, curly
   endive, lollo rosso, frisée radicchio, corn
   lettuce, watercress, etc.

Dressing:

3 tablespoons olive oil
½ tablespoon raspberry vinegar
freshly ground black pepper

Provided the leaves are really fresh, this recipe gives a good source of vitamin C. Also high in fibre.

1. Set the oven to 230°C/450°F (Gas Mark 8).
2. Mix the olive oil with the garlic and spread over the slices of bread. Place on a rack and bake in the oven for 5-8 minutes until crisp. Cut into cubes and leave to cool.
3. Place the pumpkin seeds in a heavy-based pan and cover with a lid. Toast over a high heat for about a minute or so. The lid is necessary to stop the seeds jumping out of the pan as their skins burst. Leave to cool.
4. Toss all the salad leaves together. Sprinkle with the croûtons.
5. Mix all the dressing ingredients and toss the salad in this. Sprinkle with the pumpkin seeds and serve at once.

Italian pecorino and walnut salad

Pecorino cheese is the traditional cheese used for this dish in Italy. However, if you cannot easily find any, use either Caerphilly or a firm goat's cheese in its place. Take care with the garlic. Raw garlic can taste very much stronger than cooked garlic.

8 oz (225g) Pecorino cheese, diced
4 oz (115g) walnut halves, coarsely chopped
4 tablespoons freshly chopped parsley
4 tablespoons olive oil
4 tablespoon garlic-flavoured wine vinegar
1 clove garlic, crushed
freshly ground black pepper
lettuce leaves, as required
2 slices wholemeal bread, dried in the oven and cubed

Garnish:

6–8 cherry tomatoes
sprigs of continental parsley

1. Place all the ingredients except the lettuce leaves, bread and garnishes in a bowl and mix well together.
2. Line four plates or bowls with the lettuce and spoon the Pecorino salad on the top.
3. Sprinkle with dry bread croûtons and garnish with cherry tomatoes and sprigs of parsley.

Walnuts are a good source of folic acid. Goat's cheese can be eaten by those who are allergic to cow's milk.

Kiwi salad

6 tomatoes, thinly sliced
3 kiwi fruit, peeled and sliced
2 tablespoons pinenuts, toasted
sprigs of continental parsley

Dressing:

2 tablespoons polyunsaturated salad oil
2 teaspoons lemon juice
a little grated lemon rind

1. Arrange a layer of most of the sliced tomatoes on four individual plates.
2. Add a small layer of kiwi fruit on top and finish off with the few remaining slices of tomato.
3. Sprinkle with the toasted pinenuts and decorate with sprigs of continental parsley.
4. Mix the salad oil, lemon juice and rind and pour over the top.

Serving suggestion:

Serve with Leek and hazelnut loaf (see page 125), nut roasts or in a salad medley. It also makes a good starter.

Toasted nuts

Toasting of any kinds of nuts seems to bring extra flavour out of them and this is particularly true of pinenuts.

Toast them under the grill or in a dry frying pan over a medium heat. Keep the nuts on the move to prevent them burning.

Lemons

Many lemons are treated with substances which remain on their skins — so give them a good scrub before grating.

Chinese celery and cucumber salad

I generally serve this with Chinese stir-fry dishes but it can also make a very effective contrast to nut roast.

½ small head celery, very finely chopped
½ cucumber, diced
3-4 spring onions, finely chopped
¼ green pepper, seeded and finely chopped
2 tablespoons soya sauce
3 drops sesame oil

1. Mix the celery, cucumber, spring onions and green pepper in a bowl.
2. Mix all the remaining ingredients in a cup and pour over the salad.
3. Toss well together and leave to stand for at least 15 minutes or until required.

Beetroot and raisin salad with horseradish

8 oz (225g) raw beetroot, peeled
3 spring onions, very finely chopped
1 eating apple
juice of ½ lemon
2 oz (55g) raisins
5 oz (140g) low-fat yogurt
½-1 teaspoon grated horseradish
freshly ground black pepper

1. Grate the beetroot into a bowl using the fine mesh on the grater. Stir in the spring onion.
2. Core and finely chop the apple and mix with the lemon juice at once to avoid discoloration.
3. Mix into the beetroot with all the remaining ingredients.

Very good source of vitamin C and fibre.

Horseradish

In Elizabethan times horseradish was considered to be good for the complexion. This effect was thought to be even stronger if the horseradish was mixed with vinegar!

Canadian honey slaw

6 oz (170g) white cabbage, very finely shredded
1 red skinned apple, cored and coarsely grated
2 sticks celery, cut into thin sticks, 1½ inches (4cm) long
¼ pint (140ml) soured cream or yogurt
1 tablespoon runny honey
1 tablespoon vinegar
½ teaspoon wholegrain mustard
¼ teaspoon paprika pepper

1. Mix the cabbage, apple and celery in a bowl.
2. Mix all the remaining ingredients and pour over the cabbage mixture.
3. Toss well to coat everything with the dressing.
4. For freshness serve at once. For softer texture leave to stand for ½ hour before serving.

Very good source of fibre.

Honey

Honey is made up of sugar and water. The sugars are mainly fructose and glucose with only a small amount of sucrose. Honey contains traces of various minerals but no vitamins. Comb honey also contains pollen.

Desserts

Fruit petits fours

Use any kind of mixed fruit in season.

2 oranges, peeled and segmented
1 crisp apple, cored and cut into wedges
1 peach or nectarine, stoned and cut into
  wedges
grated rind of 2 oranges
2 tablespoons wheatgerm
1 tablespoon sesame seeds, toasted
1 tablespoon chopped mixed nuts
Greek yogurt
maraschino cherries
sprigs of mint

1. Prepare all the fruit.
2. Mix the orange rind and wheatgerm together and place on a saucer.
3. Mix the sesame seeds and nuts and place on another saucer.
4. Dip each piece of fruit in yogurt and then roll in one of the two coating mixtures.
5. Arrange on a plate and serve with a few maraschino cherries and a sprig of mint.

Variations on coatings:

For special occasions add a little grated chocolate or toasted desiccated coconut to the wheatgerm.

Wheatgerm

Wheatgerm is a valuable food supplement being rich in the B complex vitamins and in vitamin E. However, it is also rich in unsaturated fatty acids and quickly goes rancid if it is not kept in the fridge.

Avocado creams

You can use honey instead of sugar but this will change the flavour somewhat and you may need to experiment with the type of honey used.

2 large avocados, peeled and stoned
juice of 2 lemons
2 tablespoons light muscovado sugar
  (optional)
½ pint (285ml) Greek yogurt

1. Mash, sieve or blend the avocados with the lemon juice to prevent discoloration. Mix with the sugar if using.
2. Next, stir in the yogurt and chill until required.

Strawberry fool

All kinds of soft fruit can be treated in this way. Try mangoes, raspberries or a mixture of very ripe gooseberries and strawberries.

12 oz (340g) strawberries
1 tablespoon lemon juice
1 tablespoon honey (optional)
1 egg, separated
4 tablespoons Greek yogurt

1. Rub the strawberries through a sieve and mix with the lemon juice, honey (if using), egg yolk and yogurt.
2. Whisk the egg white until it is very stiff. Mix a spoonful into the strawberry mixture and then fold in the rest.

Banana nut cream

Prepare all the ingredients in advance and then make this delicious but easy dessert immediately before serving it.

4 ripe bananas
juice of 1 lemon
5 oz (140g) Greek yogurt
1 oz (30g) walnuts, coarsely chopped
1 oz (30g) almonds, coarsely chopped
a little grated lemon rind

1. Mash the bananas with a fork and quickly mix with lemon juice to prevent discoloration.
2. Stir in the yogurt, nuts and lemon rind and spoon into four bowls.

Variation:

Add chopped dates, dried apricots or crunchy oat mix.

Winter fruit salad with kumquats

Pouring boiling water onto no-soak apricots plumps them up and makes them easier to eat in a fruit salad. It also cleans them.

juice of 2 oranges*
4 oz (115g) no-soak apricots
1 green-skinned apple, cored and diced
1 red-skinned apple, cored and diced
2 kiwi fruit, peeled and diced
8 kumquats, sliced

1. Pour boiling water over the apricots and leave to stand until cold. Drain and halve or quarter.
2. Mix with the diced fruits, kumquats and orange juice and serve at once.

Dried apricots retain around 50 per cent of their vitamin A content and are a good source of potassium. Vitamin C is provided by the oranges, kumquats and kiwi fruit.

* Squeeze the oranges before preparing the fruit. Each piece of fruit can then go straight into the juice. This helps to cut down on vitamin loss and discoloration.

Mango and orange sorbet

Sorbets and water ices must include either sugar or alcohol if they are not to freeze so hard that it is impossible to eat them. The choice is yours — you can vary the amounts of either or leave one out altogether.

3 oz (85g) light muscovado sugar
3 fl oz (90ml) water
1 liqueur glass orange liqueur such as
    Grand Marnier or *Cointreau*
1 pint (570ml) orange juice
a little grated orange rind
1 mango, peeled and stoned
2 egg whites

Good source of vitamin C.

1. Heat the sugar and water in a pan and stir until the sugar dissolves. Leave to cool and mix with the orange liqueur, orange juice and orange rind.
2. Purée the mango in a blender or rub through a sieve and add to the orange juice.
3. Pour into a freezer container and freeze for 2–3 hours until the liquid has begun to freeze and is quite slushy when stirred.
4. Whisk the egg whites until very stiff. Stir the slush to spread the mango purée evenly and fold in the egg whites.
5. Return to the freezer and leave for a further 4 hours.

Serving suggestions:

Keep the orange skins and clean out all the flesh. Freeze, fill with the sorbet mixture and freeze again. You may need to cut a little skin off the base so that the orange cups will not roll over when served on a plate. Alternatively they can be served in a glass.

Fruit kebabs

Other special fruits to use in season include melon balls, stoned fresh dates, peach or nectarine and slices of star fruit.

2 small bananas, peeled and cut into chunks
2 red-skinned apples, cored and cut into wedges
2 tablespoons lemon juice
8 strawberries or cherries
or
4 kumquats
2 kiwi fruit, cut into chunks
or
4 apricots, cut in half and stoned
sprigs of fresh mint

1. Dip the chunks of banana and apple into the lemon juice to prevent discoloration.
2. Choose the supporting fruit and thread onto four long or eight short skewers in an attractive pattern of colours adding some sprigs of mint from time to time. Serve at once.

Marinated oranges with rosemary

2 sprigs rosemary
2 fl oz (60ml) vermouth
3 fl oz (90ml) orange juice
4 fresh oranges, peeled and sliced
extra rosemary sprigs to garnish

1. Stand the rosemary in the vermouth and orange juice for 1 hour in the fridge.
2. Prepare the oranges and pour the liquid over the top.
3. Garnish with sprigs of rosemary.

Good source of vitamin C.

Pears with blackcurrant sauce

Frozen blackcurrants work very well in this recipe. Remember to catch all the juice as they thaw. *Cassis* enhances the natural blackcurranty taste of the sauce. *Mûre*, the French blackberry liqueur, gives a subtle mixed berry flavour.

8 oz (225g) blackcurrants
1–2 tablespoons *Crème de Cassis* or *Crème de Mûre* (optional)
raw-cane sugar, to taste
4 very ripe pears, peeled

Garnish:

sprigs of mint

Excellent source of vitamin C and good fibre content.

1. Rub most of the blackcurrants through a sieve, extracting as much pulp as possible.
2. Discard the pips and skins and mix the pulp with the *Cassis* or brandy if using. Taste and add sugar if necessary.
3. Place the peeled pears on individual plates and pour the blackcurrant purée over the top.
4. Decorate with the remaining whole fruit and sprigs of mint.

3

A TOUCH OF HEAT

Starters

Celery and apple soup

Sherry added to soup seems to give a real lift to the flavour. All the alcohol is, of course, boiled off. Vegetable water from boiling or steaming vegetables is quite strong enough for this recipe.

1 tablespoon sunflower or safflower oil
1 large onion, peeled and chopped
1-inch (2.5cm) piece fresh root ginger, peeled and grated
2 fl oz (60ml) dry sherry (optional)
12 oz (340g) cooking apples, cored and chopped
12 oz (340g) celery, chopped
½ teaspoon ground cumin powder
sea salt and freshly ground black pepper
1¾ pint (1 litre) thin vegetable stock or water
4 tablespoons soured cream or Greek yogurt

1. Heat the oil in a large saucepan and fry the onion and ginger gently for 1-2 minutes.
2. Add all the remaining ingredients except the cream or yogurt and bring to the boil.
3. Simmer for 30 minutes and then blend or rub through a sieve.
4. Serve hot or cold with a dollop of soured cream or yogurt.

Julienne miso broth

This is a good recipe for using up vegetable water left over from steaming vegetables. Add sliced tofu for a more substantial soup. Do not allow the soup to boil after the miso has been added.

1¾ pints (1 litre) weak vegetable stock
1 carrot, cut into very thin strips
1 courgette, cut into very thin strips
6 spring onions, cut in half lengthways
2 teaspoons miso

1. Bring the vegetable stock to the boil and add the vegetables. Simmer for 5–6 minutes.
2. Mix the miso with 2 or 3 tablespoons of the hot stock and stir this mixture back into the soup off the heat. Serve at once.

Stracciatelle with oyster mushrooms

This is a Roman soup but it is popular all over Italy. This version with mushrooms was served to me at a villa near Florence.

2 eggs
1 tablespoon fine semolina
2 tablespoons finely grated Parmesan cheese
1 tablespoon freshly chopped parsley
1½ pints (850ml) good vegetable stock
1 teaspoon yeast extract
3 oz (85g) oyster or shiitake mushrooms, sliced thinly

1. Beat the eggs in a bowl with the semolina, Parmesan cheese and parsley.
2. Add about 3 fl oz (90ml) of the vegetable stock and beat to a smooth cream.
3. Mix the yeast extract with a little of the remaining stock and then heat with the rest of the stock in a pan with the sliced mushrooms.
4. Bring the mixture to the boil and cook for 1 minute. Pour in the egg and semolina mixture.
5. Beat with a fork for 3–4 minutes until the broth almost returns to the boil and the eggs cook into fine shreds. Serve at once with more cheese.

Courgette and wild rice soup

This recipes comes from Canada where courgettes are known by their Italian name of Zucchini. For a good colour, use onion skins when preparing your vegetable stock.

1¾ pint (1 litre) good strong vegetable stock
2 tablespoons wild rice, well-washed in warm water
2 small courgettes, cut into thin strips
6 spring onions, sliced lengthways

Garnish:

sprigs of fresh coriander

1. Pour ¼ pint (140ml) of the stock into a saucepan and add the washed rice. Bring to the boil and simmer for 45 minutes, checking from time to time, to see that the rice has not boiled dry.
2. Leave to stand for 30 minutes off the heat. Add all the remaining stock and return to the boil.
3. Add the courgettes and spring onions and simmer for 4–5 minutes. Serve garnished with springs of fresh coriander.

Cooking wild rice

Some types of wild rice have been treated so that they can be cooked in the above manner. Others may require soaking before use. These can be soaked overnight or a quicker method is to stir into boiling water. Simmer for 5 minutes and leave to soak for 1 hour. Drain and proceed as in the recipe, cooking for about 20 minutes only.

Hot tossed cabbage

2 tablespoons raisins
2 fl oz (60ml) orange juice
a little grated orange rind
2 tablespoons cider vinegar
3 tablespoons sunflower or safflower oil
1 teaspoon whole cumin seed
1 teaspoon black or yellow mustard seed
1 onion, peeled and sliced
6 oz (170g) green cabbage, very finely shredded
3 oz (85g) red cabbage, very finely shredded

Garnish:

3 tablespoons flaked almonds, toasted

1. Place the raisins in a cup with the orange juice and rind and the vinegar.
2. Heat the cooking oil in a large frying pan or wok. Fry the whole spices for about a minute until they begin to pop.
3. Add the onion and cabbage to the pan and stir-fry over a medium heat for 3–4 minutes.
4. Pour on the raisins and orange juice and cook for a further 1–2 minutes.
5. Serve hot from the pan, garnished with the toasted flaked almonds.

Provence vegetable moulds

1 lb (455g) tomatoes, peeled and seeded
1 red pepper, seeded and chopped
1 small courgette, chopped
4 shallots or 6 spring onions, trimmed and chopped
1 teaspoon each freshly chopped rosemary, thyme and tarragon
3 fl oz (85ml) white wine or vegetable stock
2 teaspoons *Gelozone*

Garnish:

lemon twists
gherkin fans

1. Blend the vegetables, herbs and stock in a blender. Transfer to a saucepan.
2. Sprinkle the gelozone over the top and bring to the boil.
3. Stir and pour into individual moulds. Place in the fridge to set.
4. Turn out and serve garnished with lemon twists and gherkin fans.

Lemon twists:

Cut the lemon into thin slices. Make a radial cut into the centre of each slice and twist to give a spiral effect.

Good source of vitamin C. If you can find a vegetarian setting agent which does not require boiling with the liquid to be set, you would retain more of the vitamin C content.

Gherkin fans:

Cut the gherkin into slices lengthways from the tip, but avoid cutting all the way through at the stalk end. Fan out the slices.

Tofu in teryaki sauce

Tofu really has the capacity to soak up other flavours and this simple dish is quite delicious. Serve it after Miso soup, before or with a main course.

10 oz (285g) tofu
1 tablespoon sunflower seed oil
3 fl oz (85ml) light soya sauce
2 tablespoons Mirin or sweet sherry
1 tablespoon rice or other vinegar
1 teaspoon grated root ginger
2 spring onions, finely chopped

1. Cut the tofu into large rectangular pieces.
2. Heat the oil in a non-stick frying pan and fry the tofu on all sides to seal. Place in small individual bowls.
3. Heat the soya sauce, Mirin or sherry and vinegar with the ginger in a pan and pour over the tofu. Leave to cool to lukewarm.
4. Just before serving sprinkle with the chopped spring onions.

Mirin

Mirin is a sweet rice wine, available along with rice vinegar in Japanese shops. Sweet sherry can be used but the flavour is not quite the same.

Pasta with pinenuts

Freshly grated Parmesan cheese has a very much better flavour than any ready-grated version. Buy 1 lb (455g) at a time and cut into 2–3 oz (55–85g) pieces. Double wrap and store one piece in the fridge — it will keep for a month or more — and store the rest in the freezer.

8 oz (225g) green or wholemeal tagliatelle
   or noodles
sea salt
6 tablespoons olive oil
2 cloves garlic, finely chopped or crushed
2 oz (55g) pinenuts
3 oz (85g) grated Parmesan cheese
freshly ground black pepper
4 tablespoons soured cream

Garnish:

freshly chopped chervil or parsley

Good carbohydrate and fibre content. Pinenuts contain polyunsaturated fatty acids and are a good source of potassium and phosphorus.

1. Cook the noodles in a large pan of boiling salted water with a tablespoon of the oil until just tender.
2. Meanwhile heat the remaining oil gently in a small pan. Add the garlic and pinenuts and stir over a gentle heat until the nuts and garlic brown slightly.
3. Remove from the heat and stir in the Parmesan cheese.
4. Drain the cooked noodles thoroughly and toss in the nut mixture and black pepper.
5. Spoon the noodles onto a serving dish and top with the soured cream and a little freshly chopped chervil or parsley.

Sesame stuffed mushrooms

4 large or 8 medium field mushrooms,
   washed and thoroughly dried
olive oil
sesame oil
1 clove garlic, crushed
1 very small onion, very finely chopped
2 tablespoons toasted sesame seeds
2 oz (55g) fresh wholemeal breadcrumbs
3 tablespoons freshly chopped parsley
1 egg, beaten

*Good fibre content together with a good mix
of vitamins.*

1. Set the oven to 200°C/400°F (Gas
   Mark 6). Grease a medium-sized baking
   tray.
2. Remove the stalks from the mushrooms.
   Chop and place with the other
   ingredients.
3. Brush the caps with olive oil and
   sprinkle one or two drops of sesame oil
   on each cap.
4. Mix all the remaining ingredients to a
   paste with the chopped stalks. Spread a
   little over each mushroom cap.
5. Place on the prepared tray and bake for
   10–15 minutes.

Serving suggestion:

Serve on squares of toast cut to the size
of the mushroom cap. Garnish with
watercress.

Variation:

Non vegans might like to add 2
tablespoons grated Parmesan cheese for a
change.

Artichoke, tarragon and egg flans

The French refer to these savoury egg custards as flans even though there is no pastry involved. I first had these in the south west of France and they are now a popular Sunday Brunch idea.

sunflower oil
4 cooked artichoke bases
¼ pint (140ml) well-flavoured vegetable stock
½ pint (285ml) skimmed milk
2 whole eggs
1 egg yolk
sea salt and freshly ground black pepper
½ teaspoon freshly chopped tarragon or ¼ teaspoon dried tarragon
2 tablespoons freshly grated Parmesan cheese (optional)

1. Grease 4 ramekin dishes with the oil and set the oven to 180°C/350°F (Gas Mark 4).
2. Place the artichoke bases in the ramekin dishes.
3. Mix the stock and milk in a pan and bring to just before boiling point.
4. Beat the eggs with the egg yolk in a bowl and pour the hot milk over them. Beat with a fork and add the seasoning and tarragon. Pour over the artichokes. Sprinkle with cheese if using.
5. Place in a baking tray filled with 1 inch (2.5cm) hot water and bake for 30 minutes until set.

Artichokes

Buy fresh artichokes in season and trim off the leaves. Cut out most of the choke and steam in a very little salted water or in a steamer, or cook in the microwave. Use canned artichoke bases, not hearts, out of season.

Gaucho bean dip

Serve with raw vegetable crudités like carrot and cucumber sticks and cauliflower florets and with Nachos (Mexican corn chips). Take care to buy the plain Nachos, not the corn chips packaged as quick snacks. The latter often have a very nasty tasting coating to them.

1 small onion, finely chopped
1 tablespoon olive oil
1 × 9 oz (250g) tin red kidney beans, well-drained
2 oz (55g) low-fat soft cheese
6 spring onions, very finely chopped
1 green chilli, seeded and finely chopped
1 teaspoon lemon juice
1–2 tablespoons natural yogurt

Topping:

2 oz (55g) pimento stuffed olives, halved
1-inch (2.5cm) piece cucumber, sliced

Very good source of fibre and B complex vitamins, especially B_1 and B_3.

1. Fry the onion in the olive oil until soft and lightly browned. This will take 4–5 minutes.
2. Add the beans and squash down with a potato masher. Fry until lightly browned at the base. Turn over and brown the second side.
3. Leave to cool and then mix with all the remaining ingredients, adding sufficient yogurt to give a dipping texture.
4. Spoon into a bowl and smooth over the top with a spoon.
5. Decorate with stuffed olive halves and cucumber slices.

Fettucine al fredo

Serves 4 as a starter or 2 as a main course

½ lb (225g) fresh noodles, fettucine or
  tagliatelle
1 large egg, beaten
5 oz (140g) natural yogurt
2 oz (55g) freshly grated Parmesan cheese
2 fl oz (60ml) white wine
1 large knob butter or sunflower margarine
freshly grated nutmeg or dried or chopped
  oregano
freshly ground black pepper
1 medium-sized onion, very thinly chopped
6 oz (170g) frozen peas
4 tablespoons freshly chopped parsley

1. Cook the pasta for 2-3 minutes or as
   directed on the pack until al dente.
2. Whisk the egg, yogurt, cheese, wine,
   pepper, nutmeg or oregano and keep on
   one side.
3. Melt the butter or margarine and gently
   fry the onion until transparent. This only
   takes a minute or two. Add the peas and
   heat through.
4. Drain the pasta and toss in the egg and
   yogurt mixture. Add the onions and peas
   and top with parsley. Serve at once.

Variation:

Top with toasted pinenuts if serving as a
main course.

*High carbohydrate and fibre content. Good
mix of vitamins.*

Parmesan cheese

Freshly grated Parmesan always has a
much better flavour than the ready-
grated variety. Cut the fresh Parmesan
into pieces and freeze. Grate from
frozen.

Winter soups and hotpots

Swiss barley soup

Be sure to use pot barley not pearl barley, which has had much of the goodness polished off it. Vegans can use soya milk. Indeed, it's well worth trying soya milk whether you are a vegan or not — it tastes almost creamy. Remember to use some onion skins when preparing your vegetable stock — they really improve the colour.

2 oz (55g) wholegrain or pot barley, washed and well-drained
1 onion, finely chopped
1 pint (570ml) good vegetable stock
¾ pint (425ml) skimmed milk
sea salt and freshly ground black pepper

1. Place all the ingredients in a pan and bring to the boil.
2. Reduce the heat, cover and simmer for 1 hour.
3. Serve with crusty wholemeal rolls.

Thick swede and fennel soup

1 oz (30g) sunflower oil
1½ lb (680g) swede, peeled and sliced
3 oz (85g) carrot, peeled and sliced
8 oz (225g) head fennel, trimmed and sliced
1 vegetable stock cube
1¾ pints (1 litre) water
sea salt and freshly ground black pepper

1. Heat the cooking oil in a large pan. Gently sweat the vegetables over a low heat to bring out the flavour. This takes about 3-4 minutes.
2. Crumble in the stock cube and pour on the water. Bring to the boil, reduce the heat and simmer for 20–25 minutes until the vegetables are tender.
3. Purée in a blender or rub through a sieve. Season to taste.
4. Reheat and serve with Wholemeal rolls (page 28).

Lentil soup with spinach

Whole lentils may take a little longer to cook and you may need to adjust the amount of stock required.

1 large onion, sliced
1 tablespoon sunflower seed oil
1 potato, chopped
4 oz (115g) split or whole lentils
1¾ pints (1 litre) vegetable stock
¼ teaspoon ground cumin
sea salt and freshly ground black pepper
2 oz (55g) spinach

1. Fry the onion in the oil in a large pan for 4–5 minutes to brown slightly.
2. Add all the remaining ingredients except the spinach and bring to the boil. Reduce the heat and simmer for 35–40 minutes until all the vegetables are tender.
3. Purée in a blender or rub through a sieve and reheat.
4. Shred the spinach and stir into the soup. Serve almost at once.

Good source of B complex vitamins and fibre.

Potatoes

Potatoes are a good source of vitamin C. However, a good deal of this vitamin C is situated just under the skin and is often lost when potatoes are peeled. The ideal solution is to eat the skins but if this is not practicable peel the potatoes after cooking or peel very thinly indeed with a special potato peeler.

Italian bread soup

For the best flavour results this soup needs to be very well cooked indeed. Make up for any vitamin loss by following it with fruit. The soup is traditionally served with extra virgin olive oil on the side. The soup should be very thick and a little oil should be poured over the top before eating.

1 large or 2 medium leeks, trimmed and sliced
1 tablespoon olive oil
8 oz (225g) cabbage or greens, shredded
½ small cauliflower or bunch broccoli tops, cut into chunks
1 large potato, peeled and chopped
3 tomatoes, peeled and chopped
¼ pint (140ml) vegetable water or weak stock
½ small wholemeal loaf, cut into chunks

Good source of vitamin E and B complex vitamins — also high in fibre.

1. Fry the leek slices in olive oil and brown slightly. Add the cabbage and toss in the oil for 1 minute.
2. Add all the remaining vegetables and stir well. Pour on the vegetable water or stock and bring to the boil.
3. Cook for an hour until the vegetables are very well cooked and the soup is pretty thick.
4. Place the chunks of bread in the base of a large flameproof casserole dish and ladle the soup over the top. Heat gently for 3–4 minutes and serve from the pot.

Soupe au pistou

In Provence this soup is usually made with fresh white beans. However, dried and semi-cooked or tinned white haricot beans are much easier to find elsewhere. The flavour of the soup depends very much on the amount of fresh basil used so do use plenty.

1 large potato, peeled and diced
2 carrots, peeled and diced
3 tomatoes, peeled and chopped
2 leeks, trimmed and sliced into rounds
3 pints (1.8 litres) water
8 oz (225g) courgettes, sliced
3 oz (85g) French beans, cut into lengths
2 oz (55g) wholemeal macaroni or spaghetti, broken into pieces
1×8 oz (225g) tin haricot beans, drained

Pistou:

2–3 cloves garlic, chopped
1 bunch fresh basil
2 oz (55g) Parmesan cheese, freshly grated
1–2 tablespoons olive oil
sea salt and freshly ground black pepper

1. Place the potatoes, carrots, tomatoes and leeks in a pan and cover with the water. Bring to the boil and simmer for 30 minutes.
2. Add the courgettes, French beans and macaroni and cook for another 15 minutes.
3. Add the haricot beans and cook for another 5 minutes.
4. Meanwhile make the *pistou* sauce by grinding the garlic in a food processor or with a pestle and mortar with the basil leaves, adding the latter a few at a time.
5. Next add half the cheese and oil and then the rest. Season to taste.
6. Spoon the cooked soup into large bowls. Serve with the *pistou* sauce in a bowl so that everyone can help themselves.

Baked rice biryani

Biryani is an Indian dish. It is usually made for very special occasions and involves cooking the rice twice. This version is a little quicker to make as the rice is only cooked once.

1 phial saffron
¼ pint (140ml) warm milk
8 black peppercorns
4 cloves

1. Set the oven to 190°C/375°F (Gas Mark 5).
2. Mix the saffron and warm milk and keep on one side.

seeds from 4 cardamom pods
2 tablespoons sunflower seed oil
2 cloves garlic, crushed
2 tablespoons flaked almonds, chopped
2-inch (3cm) piece fresh root ginger,
  peeled and grated
2 onions, peeled and sliced
1 tablespoon ground cumin
1 tablespoon ground coriander
a little grated nutmeg
2 lb (900g) mixed vegetables,* peeled and
  chopped
10 oz (285g) yogurt
4 hard-boiled eggs, halved or quartered
8 oz (225g) brown rice
½ pint (285ml) boiling vegetable stock

Garnish:

1 onion, sliced
1 tablespoon cooking oil
1 tablespoon raisins
2 tablespoons toasted almonds

3. Fry the whole spices in the cooking oil
   for about one minute. Add the garlic,
   almonds, ginger and onions and fry for
   4–5 minutes until lightly browned.
4. Stir in the spices, mixed vegetables and
   yogurt and bring to the boil. Cover and
   reduce the heat and cook for 15
   minutes.
5. Layer with the eggs and brown rice in
   an ovenproof dish. Pour on the boiling
   stock and stir carefully.
6. Pour on the saffron milk and bake for 1
   hour 10 minutes. Turn off the heat and
   leave to stand in a warm place for 10
   minutes.
7. Meanwhile make the garnish by frying
   the onion in the oil until very well
   browned, adding the raisins about half
   way through.
8. Scatter over the top of the biryani with
   the toasted almonds just before serving.

Serving suggestions:

This is a filling dish and only needs the
addition of a runny dahl or a well dressed
salad to complete the meal.

* Use any vegetables in season. A mixture of carrots, courgettes, mushrooms and peppers works very well, but
almost any vegetable to hand can be used. Try peas or beans, fennel, swede or celery.

Polenta pie

8 oz (225g) courgettes, thinly sliced
6 tomatoes, peeled and sliced
4 spring onions, finely chopped
4 oz (115g) firm cheese, grated
¼ teaspoon oregano
sea salt and freshly ground black pepper
3 oz (85g) yellow cornmeal or polenta
18 fl oz (510ml) water
1 oz (30g) butter or firm margarine
1 oz (30g) grated Parmesan cheese

Choose yellow cornmeal for its vitamin A content rather than white cornmeal. Reasonable source of vitamin B complex and vitamin C.

1. Layer the courgettes, tomatoes, spring onions and cheese in a pie dish sprinkling with oregano and seasoning as you go.
2. Mix the cornmeal with half the water. Boil the remaining water in a pan.
3. Add the cornmeal and water mixture beating all the time with a wooden spoon.
4. Add the butter and plenty of salt and continue stirring until the mixture thickens and boils. Leave to simmer over a low heat for 15 minutes, stirring from time to time.
5. Spoon the cooked cornmeal over the vegetables in the pie dish and leave to stand for 15 minutes.
6. Set the oven to 200°C/400°F (Gas Mark 6). Sprinkle the top of the pie with grated Parmesan and bake for 30 minutes.
7. Serve with salad or hot tossed cabbage.

Tofu djuvec

This vegetarian variation on a mid-European favourite works well with both smoked and unsmoked tofu.

1 large onion, peeled and sliced
2 tablespoons sunflower seed oil
2 potatoes, peeled and cubed
4 green peppers, seeded and chopped
1 green chilli, seeded and chopped
  (optional)
sea salt and freshly ground black pepper
8 oz (225g) smoked or unsmoked tofu
4 oz (115g) long grain brown rice
2 oz (55g) frozen peas
4 tomatoes, peeled and chopped
4 fl oz (115ml) vegetable stock
4 tablespoons freshly chopped parsley

1. Set the oven to 190°C/375°F (Gas Mark 5).
2. Fry the onion in the cooking oil and add the potatoes, peppers and chilli if using. Gently sauté for 10 minutes and then add all the remaining ingredients.
3. Transfer to a casserole and bake for 1¼–1½ hours until the rice and potatoes are tender.
4. Sprinkle each portion with plenty of freshly chopped parsley.

Herby beanpot

7 fl oz (200ml) soya milk
2 tablespoons freshly chopped parsley
1 tablespoon freshly chopped chives
1 sprig tarragon or rosemary
1×11 oz (300g) tin butter beans
1×14½ oz (410g) tin haricot beans
4 oz (115g) frozen broad beans
½ oz (15g) butter or firm margarine
½ oz (15g) flour
sea salt and freshly ground black pepper

1. Heat the soya milk to lukewarm and stir in all the herbs except the tarragon or rosemary. Leave to stand until required.
2. Add the tarragon or rosemary to the milk 5 minutes before using and then remove.
3. Mix the beans in a pan and toss over a low heat to warm through.
4. Melt the butter in a pan and stir in the flour and the herb soya milk. Bring to the boil, stirring all the time.
5. Add the beans and make sure that the mixture is well heated.
6. Serve with crusty French bread.

Sage and apple beanpot

For a much quicker casserole substitute double the quantity of tinned beans and chick peas and use a little less liquid.

4 oz (115g) dried haricot or black eye
  beans or a mixture of the two
4 oz (115g) dried chick peas
5 fl oz (140ml) vegetable stock
1 small onion, finely chopped
½ oz (15g) butter
1 lb (455g) cooking apples, cored and
  grated
½ teaspoon yeast extract
½ teaspoon dried sage
½ teaspoon mixed dried herbs
freshly ground black pepper

Very good source of fibre and B complex vitamins, especially B_1 and B_3.

1. Soak the beans and chick peas in the vegetable stock. Leave to stand overnight in the fridge.
2. Next day, sauté the onion in the butter until lightly browned.
3. Drain the beans, reserving the liquid, and stir them into the mixture, with the apples.
4. Dissolve the yeast extract in a little of the bean water and add to the bean mixture with the herbs and pepper. Spoon into a casserole dish and add more bean water to about half way to three quarters of the way up the beans. Use any remaining water in soups.
5. Set the oven to 180°C/350°F (Gas Mark 4). Cover the pot and bake for 20 minutes until the beans are tender and most of the liquid has been taken up.

The star turn

Steamed Chinese dim sum _____

32 wonton wrappers

Filling 1:

4 oz (115g) fresh tofu
1 teaspoon freshly grated root ginger
2 spring onions, finely chopped
¼ teaspoon five spice powder

Filling 2:

4 oz (115g) smoked tofu
1 tablespoon sweet and sour sauce
2 spring onions, finely chopped
a little grated lemon rind

1. Place all the ingredients for filling 1 in a basin and mix well.
2. Place a teaspoonful on a wonton wrapper and wrap up into a small parcel. Damp and pinch the pastry to make it stick together.
3. Continue in the same way to make 16 dumplings.
4. Mix the ingredients for filling 2 in another basin and proceed as before.
5. Place all the dumplings in a steamer and steam for 20–25 minutes until the wrappers are cooked through.

Carrots with tarragon cream

2 lb (900g) whole carrots
4 teaspoons cornflour
¾ pint (425ml) skimmed milk
6 oz (170g) low-fat soft cheese
1 tablespoon freshly chopped tarragon
sea salt and freshly ground black pepper

Good source of vitamin A.

1. Set the oven to 200°C/400°F (Gas Mark 6).
2. Wrap the carrots individually in lightly-oiled foil and bake for about 50–60 minutes depending on size of the carrots.
3. Mix the cornflour with a little of the milk to form a smooth cream and then mix with the rest of the milk.
4. Beat in the cheese and pour the mixture into a pan. Bring to the boil, stirring all the time.
5. Stir in the tarragon and seasoning. Turn off the heat.
6. Remove the carrots from their foil wrappings and slice. Pour the tarragon cream over the top and serve at once.

Mushroom kebabs with Satay sauce

Although the mushrooms are the mainstay of the recipe you can change any of the other ingredients to include cherry tomatoes, baby onions, green peppers or fennel, for example. Add 1 tablespoon of creamed coconut to enrich and flavour the sauce but remember that you are adding saturated fat!

12 oz (340g) cup mushrooms, wiped clean
8 oz (225g) courgettes, cut into 1-inch (2.5cm) lengths
3 oz (85g) baby corn on the cob
1 red pepper, seeded and cut into squares
3 tablespoons sunflower or safflower oil
3 tablespoons lemon juice
1 tablespoon fresh chopped coriander
1 tablespoon chopped parsley

Satay sauce:

1 small onion, finely chopped
1 clove garlic, crushed
2 tablespoons sunflower or safflower oil
2 tablespoons smooth or crunchy peanut butter
¼ pint (140ml) vegetable stock
2 tablespoons soya sauce
a few drops Tabasco sauce

1. Place the vegetables in a large bowl. Mix the oil and lemon juice and pour over the top.
2. Sprinkle with the chopped herbs. Stir from time to time and leave to marinate for 2 hours.
3. Thread the vegetables onto skewers and cook over the barbecue or under a medium grill for 6–8 minutes, turning from time to time.
4. To make the sauce fry the onion and garlic in the cooking oil. Stir in the peanut butter and the remaining ingredients.
5. Bring to the boil and simmer for 5 minutes. Serve with the kebabs.

Good source of vitamin B complex and vitamin C, also some vitamin E. High fibre content.

Tofu and pepper kebabs

Serves 4

These colourful kebabs can be made with fresh or smoked tofu.

8 oz (225g) fresh or smoked tofu
2 tablespoons cooking oil
2 green peppers
2 red peppers

Excellent source of vitamin C. Check that the peppers are as fresh as possible. Their vitamin C content can vary five-fold!

1. Cut the tofu block into cubes about ¾–1-inch square and fry all over in the cooking oil.
2. Cut the peppers in half and remove the stalks, seeds and membranes. Cut into squares and parboil in boiling water for 4 minutes.
3. Thread pieces of tofu onto the skewers with two pieces of red or green pepper on either side of them. For example the pattern might be red pepper, tofu, red pepper, green pepper, tofu, green pepper, red pepper, tofu, red pepper.
4. Place on the barbecue or under the grill for 5–6 minutes, turning from time to time, until the peppers are cooked and the tofu has browned on the outside.

Tofu

Fresh pressed tofu can be bought in most health food shops these days. It may also be known as bean curd in Chinese shops. There is also a smoked version. If you do not use all the tofu at once it can be kept in the fridge in a bowl of water. Change the water every day.

Silken tofu comes in UHT long-life packs. It is softer and more delicate than fresh tofu. It is more difficult to cut and fry but it is easier to mix into soups, quiches and any recipe where it might take the place of soft cheese.

Mixed greens stir-fry with caraway

2 tablespoons sunflower seed oil
½ teaspoon whole caraway seeds
¼ head white cabbage, finely shredded
6 tablespoons vegetable stock
5–6 large green cabbage leaves, shredded
1 tablespoon raisins
1 little gem lettuce, shredded

Good source of vitamin A and C and also the B complex vitamins including folic acid.

1. Heat the oil in a large frying pan or wok and stir-fry the seeds for ½ minute.
2. Add the white cabbage and stir-fry for 2 minutes.
3. Add the stock and bring to the boil. Cook over a high heat to reduce the liquid by half or more.
4. Reduce the heat and add the green cabbage and raisins. Stir-fry for a further 1½–2 minutes.
5. Add the lettuce. Toss all the ingredients together well and serve at once.

Tofu and pepper stir-fry

You can ring the changes on this really quick recipe by using different vegetables in season and choosing a different stir-fry sauce each time. Just check the ingredients on the pack to make sure they do not contain animal products or too many additives. Serve with brown rice or wholemeal noodles.

2 tablespoons sunflower seed oil
1 onion, peeled and sliced
1 red pepper, seeded and cut into strips
3 oz (85g) French beans, topped and tailed
8 oz (225g) fresh tofu, cut into strips
3 oz (85g) button mushrooms, sliced
1×8 oz (225g) pack Hoisin stir-fry sauce

1. Heat the oil in a large non-stick frying pan or wok.
2. Add the onion, peppers and beans and stir-fry over a high heat for 2 minutes.
3. Add all the remaining ingredients and cook for a further 1–1½ minutes until the sauce boils. Serve at once.

Stir-fried eggs with beans

The origins of this dish lie not in China but in Italy. Courgettes cut into sticks can be treated in just the same way as the beans.

2 tablespoons olive oil
½ bunch spring onions, finely chopped
12 oz (340g) French beans, topped and tailed
4 tablespoons vegetable stock
2 eggs, beaten
sea salt and freshly ground black pepper
3 tablespoons freshly chopped parsley

1. Heat the olive oil in a non-stick wok or large frying pan and stir-fry the onions and beans for 2 minutes.
2. Add the stock and continue cooking for a minute or so until most of the stock has evaporated.
3. Pour on the eggs and continue to stir-fry for abut 2 minutes until the eggs set. Toss well with the parsley and serve.

N.B. It is essential to use a non-stick pan for this dish or the eggs will stick badly.

Leek and peas with Halloumi cheese

Halloumi cheese does not run but if it is cooked for too long it will toughen up — so take care.

3 tablespoons polyunsaturated cooking oil
1½ lb (680g) leeks, trimmed and sliced
4 oz (115g) frozen peas
2 fl oz (60ml) vermouth or vegetable stock
3 drops sesame oil
6 oz (170g) Halloumi cheese, cut into strips
freshly ground black pepper

Good mix of vitamins including A, B complex, C and D and good fibre content. Halloumi cheese is made with ewe's milk and should be suitable for those who are allergic to cow's milk.

1. Heat 2 tablespoons of the oil in a non-stick wok or large frying pan. Add the leeks and stir-fry for 1 minute.
2. Add the peas and stir-fry for a further minute.
3. Add the vermouth and sesame oil and return quickly to the boil. Continue cooking and tossing the vegetables over a light heat for 1–2 minutes until most of the liquid has evaporated.
4. Transfer to a plate and keep warm.
5. Add the remaining oil to the pan and stir-fry the cheese for about a minute. Transfer to the dish with the leeks and peas and sprinkle with black pepper. Serve at once.

Serving suggestion:

Serve with Carroty noodles (see page 92) or Ritzy rice (see page 96).

Tofu barbecue burgers

Makes 8 burgers.

Ideal for vegans and lacto-vegetarians alike, these light moist burgers can be flavoured with thyme and lemon rind for a European flavour or ground cumin, garlic and fresh coriander for a touch of the Orient.

1 onion, finely chopped
1 carrot, finely grated
2 tablespoons cooking oil
4 oz (115g) split orange lentils, cleaned
3 oz (85g) fresh wholemeal breadcrumbs
6 oz (170g) fresh tofu, mashed
1½ teaspoons fresh thyme and a little
  grated lemon rind
or
1 teaspoon freshly chopped coriander,
½ teaspoon ground cumin and 1 clove
  garlic
sea salt and freshly ground black pepper
2 tablespoons fresh wholemeal
  breadcrumbs
2 teaspoons sesame seeds

1. Soften the onion and carrot in a saucepan in hot cooking oil and then add the cleaned lentils.
2. Just cover with water. Bring to the boil and simmer for 1 hour until very dry.
3. Cool a little and then mix in the breadcrumbs, tofu and chosen herbs. Season to taste if required.
4. Place in the fridge and chill for 1 hour. Shape the cold mixture into 8 burgers.
5. Mix the breadcrumbs and sesame seeds and press onto the flat surfaces of the burgers.
6. Place 2–3 inches (5–7cm) away from the coals and grill for 4 minutes on each side.

Cooking note:

Cook under a medium grill or place on a barbecue as described. Serve with tomato or mustard sauce.

Orange and carrot cheesecake

Gelozone is quite easy to work with provided that it is added to a large quantity of liquid. Sprinkle over the top and then bring to the boil, stirring all the time. Make sure that all parts of the mixture have reached boiling point. Do not leave to cool for too long before adding to the biscuit base or it will start to get a skin on the top.

8 unsweetened wholemeal biscuits
2 oz (55g) ground hazelnuts
2 oz (55g) butter or firm polyunsaturated margarine, melted
6 oz (170g) cottage cheese
3 oz (85g) quark or fromage frais
¼ pint (140ml) unsweetened orange juice
grated rind of 1 orange
1 tablespoon lemon juice
4 oz (115g) carrot, peeled and very finely grated
1 teaspoon freshly chopped tarragon or ½ teaspoon dried tarragon
6 tablespoons wine or vegetable stock
sea salt and freshly ground black pepper
3 teaspoons *Gelozone*

1. Crush the biscuits and mix with the hazelnuts and melted fat. Press well down into the base of a 7-inch (17.5cm) loose-based cake tin. Place in the fridge to set.
2. Place the cottage cheese, quark or fromage frais, orange juice and rind and lemon juice in a food processor or blender and blend until smooth.
3. Stir in the carrot, tarragon and wine or stock and season to taste.
4. Transfer to a saucepan. Sprinkle the *Gelozone* over the top and bring to the boil whisking all the time.
5. Leave to cool a little and pour into the prepared flan tin. Leave in the fridge to set.
6. Take the cheesecake out of the flan tin and cut into wedges. Garnish with mixed salad leaves and a cherry tomato.

Fast fillers

Tomato bread with hot winter vegetable salad

If fresh basil is not available use freshly chopped parsley, chervil or tarragon. Do not use dried basil. This is one of the herbs that does not dry well and the flavour is quite different.

1 stick wholemeal French bread
8 tomatoes, peeled
1 clove garlic, cut in half
2–3 tablespoons olive oil
4 tablespoons freshly chopped basil
sea salt and freshly ground black pepper

Hot winter vegetable salad:

3 tablespoons olive oil
2 carrots, peeled and sliced on the slant
1 head fennel, thinly sliced
4 oz (115g) Chinese beansprouts
4–5 large Chinese leaves, sliced
½ bunch watercress
grated rind and juice of ½ lemon
1 teaspoon tarragon vinegar
3 tablespoons vegetable stock

1. Cut the bread into thick slices and dry out by placing under a medium to low grill for a minute or two each side. Do not allow to brown too much.
2. Meanwhile chop the tomatoes and crush with a fork.
3. Rub each piece of bread with the cut clove of garlic. Brush with oil and spread with tomato.
4. Place under the grill for a further ½ minute or so to heat through. Sprinkle with basil and serve with the salad.
5. Heat the oil in a large frying pan or wok and stir-fry the carrots and fennel for 3 minutes.
6. Add all the remaining ingredients and toss together over a high heat for ½ minute. Serve at once.

Sesame pitta bread

These crisp pitta fingers are particularly scrumptious made with butter but olive oil works well, too. Make plenty, for you will find they disappear rapidly. They are particularly good with mousses, pâtés and dips.

3 flat wholemeal pitta breads

1. Set the oven to 230°C/450°F (Gas

2 oz (55g) melted butter or 2 fl oz (60ml) olive oil
2 tablespoons sesame seeds
sea salt

Mark 8).
2. Brush the pitta bread with plenty of melted butter or olive oil and place on a baking tray. Sprinkle the top with sesame seeds.
3. Cut into long thin strips and bake for about 4–5 minutes until crisp and golden. Serve with any meal which requires bread on the side.

Corn and soya milk drop scones

If you do not have self-raising flour to hand use ordinary wholemeal flour and add 2½ teaspoons baking powder.

8 oz (225g) wholemeal self-raising flour
½ teaspoon cream of tartar
¼ teaspoon sea salt
2 eggs
½ pint (285ml) soya milk
6 oz (170g) cooked sweetcorn kernels
polyunsaturated cooking oil

Good source of magnesium and iron plus vitamin E.

1. Mix the flour, cream of tartar and salt and beat in the eggs and a little of the soya milk to form a smooth cream. Beat in the rest of the soya milk and the corn.
2. Brush a heavy frying pan or griddle with a little oil. Heat the pan and drop in spoonfuls of the mixture.
3. Cook on one side for a minute or two until bubbles appear on the surface and the base is lightly browned. Turn over and cook on the second side.
4. Keep warm until all the mixture has been used up.

Serving suggestion:

Serve with Mixed greens stir-fry (page 85) or with one of the soups.

Carroty noodles

Use either dried egg noodles or the 'cellophane' transparent noodles made from rice. If you prefer to stick to wholefoods the recipe works equally well with cooked buckwheat noodles or wholemeal spaghetti.

6 oz (170g) Chinese noodles
3 tablespoons polyunsaturated cooking oil
6–8 whole coriander seeds
3 large carrots, peeled and grated coarsely
1 white turnip, peeled and grated coarsely (optional)
1 tablespoon soya sauce
2 tablespoons dry sherry or dry vermouth
freshly ground black pepper

Good source of vitamin A. If wholewheat spaghetti is used, also high in vitamin E and fibre.

1. Cook the noodles as directed on the pack.
2. Heat 1 tablespoon of the oil in a non-stick wok or large frying pan and fry the coriander seeds for ½ minute or so.
3. Add the carrots and turnip (if using) and stir-fry for 1–2 minutes. Remove the vegetables from the pan.
4. Add the rest of the oil and the noodles. Toss over a medium heat for one minute.
5. Now return the vegetables to the pan with the soya sauce, sherry or vermouth and pepper. Toss everything together well and serve.

Herb-tossed tagliatelle

Shredded spinach, sorrel or lovage leaves can be used in place of the herbs in this recipe.

1 clove garlic, finely chopped
4 tablespoons roughly chopped parsley
4 tablespoons olive oil
2 oz (55g) chopped walnuts
12 oz (340g) tagliatelle
3 tablespoons white wine or vegetable stock
1 large bunch fresh chives, watercress or
 basil, chopped

Garnish:

freshly grated Parmesan cheese (optional)

*High carbohydrate content and good
vitamin C. If watercress is the chosen herb,
serve with a tomato salad to help the
absorption of iron.*

1. Gently fry the garlic and parsley in the olive oil. After about a minute add the walnuts and cook for a further minute but do not brown.
2. Leave on one side and cook the pasta as directed on the pack. Drain very well and place in a heated bowl.
3. Add the stock or white wine to the nut mixture and return to the boil.
4. Add the chopped herbs and pour over the pasta. Toss well together.
5. Serve sprinkled with grated Parmesan cheese, if liked.

Coriander pasta

The easiest way to cut thin strips of rind from an orange is to use a special cannelling knife.

For a special occasion pour ¼ pint (140ml) double cream into the frying pan and bring to the boil before adding the coriander and leeks to the pasta.

12 oz (340g) wholemeal spaghetti,
   tagliatelle or pasta shapes
sea salt
1 teaspoon olive oil
1 tablespoon whole coriander seeds
2 tablespoons olive oil
12 oz (340g) leeks, trimmed and sliced
   into thin rounds
thin strips of orange rind, cut from 1
   orange
sea salt and freshly ground black pepper

High carbohydrate and fibre content.

1. Cook the pasta in plenty of boiling salted water with 1 teaspoon of olive oil.
2. Meanwhile fry the whole coriander seeds in hot olive oil for about a minute until they begin to pop.
3. Add the leeks and orange rind and quickly stir-fry for about a minute or so until they just begin to soften.
4. Drain the pasta very well and place in a large bowl. Add the leek mixture and toss well together. Season to taste.

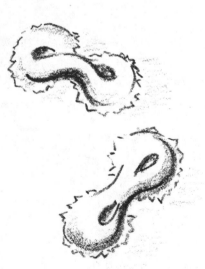
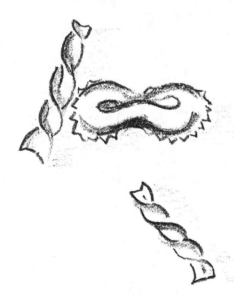

Fettucine with fennel and tomato

1 onion, thinly sliced
2 tablespoons olive oil
2 heads fennel, cut into chunks
1½ lb (680g) tomatoes, peeled
2 tablespoons tomato purée
4 tablespoons dry vermouth or vegetable
  stock
½ teaspoon mixed dried herbs
12 oz (340g) fettucine

Garnish:

freshly ground black pepper

1. Fry the onion in 1 tablespoon of olive oil for 2–3 minutes. Add the fennel and continue frying gently for a further 2–3 minutes.
2. Add all the remaining ingredients except the pasta and bring to the boil. Simmer for 10 minutes.
3. Meanwhile cook the pasta in boiling salted water until just cooked or *al dente*. Drain very well and toss in the remaining oil.
4. Serve topped with the fennel and tomato sauce and freshly ground black pepper.

Cooking pasta

Dried pasta usually has cooking instructions on the pack. Fresh pasta cooks much more quickly — usually in 2 or 3 minutes, so start testing soon after adding to the water

Ritzy rice

Simple vegetable water will be fine for this recipe.

6 oz (170g) brown rice
4 fl oz (115ml) orange juice
a little grated orange rind
½ pint (285ml) vegetable stock
1 tablespoon cooking oil
6 spring onions, finely chopped
3 oz (85g) baby sweetcorn
1 small carrot, peeled and cut on the slant
3 oz (85g) asparagus spears, cut into
  lengths
3 oz (85g) mangetout
3 tablespoons dry white wine
¼ teaspoon five spice powder

High carbohydrate and fibre content.

1. Place the rice in a saucepan with the orange juice and rind and the vegetable stock. Bring to the boil. Stir once, cover and simmer for 25–30 minutes until all the liquid has evaporated and the rice is cooked. Leave to stand off the heat for five minutes.
2. Heat the cooking oil in a large frying pan or wok and stir-fry the spring onions, sweetcorn, carrots and asparagus for 1 minute.
3. Add the mangetout, wine and five spice powder and continue to stir-fry over a high heat for 2 minutes.
4. Stir the still crisp vegetables into the brown rice and serve at once.

Exotic rice

8 oz (225g) long-grain brown rice
2 oz (55g) dried figs, chopped
1 oz (30g) raisins
1 oz (30g) desiccated coconut
pinch cinnamon
1 pint (570ml) soya milk

1. Mix the rice with the dried fruits, coconut and cinnamon.
2. Pour the milk over the top and bring to the boil. Stir once and cover with a lid.
3. Reduce the heat and simmer for 25–30 minutes until the rice is tender and all the liquid has been absorbed.
4. Fluff up with a fork and serve.

Oven-baked rice

This and other top-of-the-stove rice and cereal dishes can be cooked in the oven. Simply bring the liquid to the boil before pouring over the rice and other ingredients in a casserole. Cover and bake at 190°C/375°F (Gas Mark 5) for about 50–60 minutes.

Dried figs

Dried figs are very rich in fibre. Weight for weight they contain almost twice as much fibre as wholemeal bread.

Wild mushroom risotto

Italian risotto rice is the only rice which will give the correct texture for this dish. However, if you feel you must use brown rice, add more stock as you go. Any kind of well-flavoured mushrooms can be used. Try a mixture of dried and fresh. The former will need to be soaked in boiling water before using.

3 tablespoons olive oil
1 small onion, peeled and finely chopped
8 oz (225g) risotto rice
1 wine glass dry white wine
1¼ pints (710ml) well-flavoured vegetable stock, at boiling point
8 oz (225g) wild mushrooms, sliced
¼ teaspoon dried thyme or oregano
2 oz (55g) Parmesan cheese

High carbohydrate content.

1. Heat 1 tablespoon of the oil in a pan and fry the onion until golden. This will take 2–3 minutes.
2. Stir in the rice and make sure it is well coated with oil.
3. Add the wine and boil briskly until it is reduced by half. Add ½ pint (285ml) stock.
4. Simmer the rice, stirring occasionally. After about 10 minutes add another ½ pint (285ml) stock and continue cooking for a further 10–15 minutes.
5. Add the remaining stock and continue cooking, stirring more frequently, until the rice is cooked and the mixture creamy but not sticky.
6. Meanwhile sauté the mushrooms in the remaining oil with the herbs. Quickly stir into the risotto and sprinkle with Parmesan cheese.

Millet pilaff

If you prefer to use whole lentils they will need to be soaked overnight and then drained before use. If you like a 'hotter' pilaff, add a seeded and finely-chopped green chilli to the onion.

8 oz (225g) whole millet
1 tablespoon cooking oil
1 teaspoon whole cumin seeds
1 teaspoon whole coriander seeds
1 small onion, finely chopped
2 oz (55g) sweetcorn kernels
2 oz (55g) frozen peas
2 oz (55g) split lentils
18 fl oz (515ml) vegetable stock

Good carbohydrate and fibre content plus B complex vitamins.

1. Dry fry the millet in a hot non-stick frying pan until well toasted. Remove from the pan and keep on one side.
2. Heat the oil in a deep pan and fry the cumin and coriander seeds for about a minute until they begin to pop.
3. Add the onion and fry for 2–4 minutes until lightly-browned. Add the remaining vegetables, lentils and the toasted millet.
4. Stir and cover with stock. Bring to the boil, stir again and reduce the heat as low as possible. Simmer very gently for 30 minutes.
5. Check to see if the millet and lentils are cooked. If not continue to cook for a further 5–10 minutes.
6. Turn off the heat and leave to stand for 5 minutes before serving.

N.B. Check after 30 minutes and adjust as necessary. You may need to add a little more stock. The millet cooks quite quickly but the lentils may take up all the stock and so slow the total cooking time for the whole dish.

Millet pilaff with lentils

8 oz (225g) whole millet
2 tablespoons sunflower seed oil
1 teaspoon cumin seeds
1 small onion, finely chopped
1 clove garlic, finely chopped
3 oz (85g) split lentils
1 pint (570ml) vegetable stock

High carbohydrate and fibre content plus vitamins B_1 and B_3.

1. Dry fry the millet in a hot non-stick frying pan until well toasted all over. Remove from the pan and keep on one side.
2. Heat the oil in the pan and fry the cumin seeds for 1 minute. Add the onion, garlic and fry until lightly browned.
3. Stir in the millet and lentils, add the stock and bring to the boil. Stir once and cover with a lid.
4. Reduce the heat and simmer very gently for 30 minutes. Check to see if more liquid is required. Stir once and continue cooking for 10–15 minutes until the vegetables are fully cooked.
5. Remove from the heat and leave to stand for 5 minutes with the lid on. Fluff up with a fork and serve.

N.B. Millet tends to take up water very quickly, so keep the heat as low as possible and check from time to time that it is not drying out.

Bulghur with ginger and apricot

12 oz (340g) cracked wheat or bulghur
water
6 oz (170g) silken tofu
4 oz (115g) no-soak dried apricots
2 lumps stem ginger in syrup, finely
  chopped
2 oz (55g) pine kernels, chopped
¼ teaspoon ground cinnamon
1 tablespoon olive oil

High carbohydrate and fibre content plus
B complex vitamins and vitamins A and C.

1. Set the oven to 180°C/350°F (Gas
   Mark 4).
2. Place the bulghur in a large bowl and
   more than cover with water. Leave to
   stand for 20 minutes. Drain and squeeze
   dry.
3. Mix with all the remaining ingredients
   and spoon into a shallow ovenproof dish.
4. Flatten the top and bake for 30 minutes.

Serving suggestion:

Serve as a main dish with Courgettes in
lemon cheese mousse (see page 122) and
salad or Provence-style corn (page 128)
and a Beanpot (see pages 79-80).

4
PACKED FOR ENERGY

Sandwich scene

Blue Brie and celery cream

4 oz (115g) Blue Brie, with the rind
  removed
2 tablespoons quark or low-fat soft cheese
2 centre sticks celery, very finely chopped
pinch celery salt
¼ teaspoon paprika pepper
8 slices wholemeal bread

1. Mash the Blue Brie and mix to a smooth
   thick cream with the quark. Stir in the
   celery and seasoning.
2. Spread over half the slices of bread and
   top with the others.

Piquant sandwich spread

Use the spread to make 3 sandwiches with lettuce leaves or sliced tomatoes or use on canapés.
Good bases include rounds of pumpernickel or rice crackers.

3 oz (85g) mild English cheese, grated
1 tablespoon grated onion
1 large gherkin, very finely chopped
1 teaspoon capers, chopped
5 tablespoons mayonnaise

1. Place all the ingredients in a basin and
   mix together well.

Banana and date spread

To keep sandwiches in their best condition wrap first in foil and then in shrink wrap. Pack into a polythene box for extra protection.

2 ripe bananas
8 dates, finely chopped
1 teaspoon lemon juice
a little grated orange rind
8 slices wholemeal bread, buttered
sprigs of fresh mint

1. Mash the bananas with a fork and mix with the dates, lemon juice and grated orange rind.
2. Spread this mixture over the slices of bread.
3. Dot with sprigs of fresh mint and cover with the remaining bread.

Tahini special

1 bunch watercress, chopped
2 tablespoons tahini
sea salt and freshly ground black pepper
1–2 beetroot, sliced
6 slices wholemeal bread, buttered

1. Mix the watercress and tahini in a basin and season to taste.
2. Arrange slices of beetroot on a slice of bread. Top with some of the watercress and tahini mixture and finish off with another slice of bread.
3. Continue with the rest of the ingredients.

Sesame and chutney sandwich spread

1 heaped tablespoon mango chutney
1 tablespoon sesame seeds
4 oz (115g) low-fat soft cheese
freshly ground black pepper

1. Chop the mango chutney finely.
2. Toast the sesame seeds until well-browned and mix with the chutney.
3. Stir this mixture into the soft cheese and season with pepper to taste.
4. Make into sandwiches with sliced cucumber or beetroot. Ring the changes by adding a little ground cumin or mild curry powder.

Peanut and garlic pâté

3 tablespoons peanut butter
4 oz (115g) soft cheese or tofu
2 cloves garlic, finely chopped
2 tablespoons yogurt or soured cream
a few drops Tabasco sauce
freshly ground black pepper

1. Carefully combine the peanut butter and soft cheese and then stir in all the remaining ingredients.
2. Make up into sandwiches with wholemeal French bread sticks and watercress

Carrot and cheese delight

This was my favourite sandwich filling as a child. You can ring the changes by using various different kinds of cheese such as Red Leicester, Wensleydale or a mixture of blue and white Stilton

6 small gherkins, very finely chopped
6 stuffed olives, very finely chopped
12 oz (340g) firm cheese, grated
1 large carrot (8 oz/225g), peeled and grated
pinch dried mixed herbs
½ teaspoon wholegrain mustard
a little yogurt

1. Place the gherkins, olives, cheese, carrot and mixed herbs in a bowl and mix together well.
2. Add the mustard and sufficient yogurt to gind the mixture together.
3. Hollow out 4 wholemeal rolls and use the mixture to fill them up. Replace the lid and wrap up in foil to travel.

Excellent source of vitamin A plus B complex vitamins and vitamin D.

Egg and onion

Makes 6 rounds using a medium-sized loaf

The traditional Jewish version of this extremely tasty sandwich filling only adds onion to the eggs, but I think that the mixture of onion and cress is rather better.

Use very finely chopped onion when spring onions are not available but remember that they can have a very strong flavour.

4 eggs
4–6 small spring onions, finely chopped
2 tablespoons mayonnaise
½ box cress

1. Hard boil the eggs and leave to cool in cold water. Shell the eggs and chop finely with a knife or mash with a fork.
2. Add the onions and mayonnaise and chill for 30 minutes if possible. Stir in the cress just before using.
3. Make into sandwiches with wholemeal bread and lettuce leaves.

Tub salads

Cucumber and cabbage slaw

1 tablespoon raisins
2 tablespoons orange juice
2 oz (55g) red cabbage, shredded
2 oz (55g) white cabbage, shredded
2-inch (5cm) piece cucumber, grated
1 tablespoon olive oil
1 teaspoon cider vinegar

1. Soak the raisins in the orange juice for an hour or so before using.
2. Mix the shredded cabbage with the cucumber and orange soaked raisins.
3. Mix the olive oil and vinegar together and pour over the salad.

White fiesta bean salad

6 oz (170g) cooked haricot beans
1 large stick celery, sliced diagonally
4 small spring onions, chopped
½ small green pepper, sliced
2 teaspoons capers (optional)
10 cherry tomatoes, halved
2 tablespoons vegetable oil
½ tablespoon vinegar
¼ teaspoon dry mustard powder
sea salt and paprika pepper

1. Combine the cooked beans, celery, onions, green pepper, capers (if using) and tomatoes in a large bowl.
2. Mix the remaining ingredients together and pour over the bean mixture. Mix well.

Millet and watercress salad with peppers

3 oz (85g) whole millet
6 fl oz (170g) water
sea salt
1 bunch watercress, coarsely chopped
½ green pepper, seeded and finely chopped
½ red pepper, seeded and finely chopped
1 green chilli, seeded and finely chopped
2 tablespoons olive oil
1 teaspoon cider vinegar

1. Pour the millet into boiling salted water. Stir once and cover with a lid.
2. Reduce the heat and simmer very gently for about 20 minutes until all the liquid has been absorbed and the millet is tender. Leave to cool.
3. Fluff up the millet and mix with all the remaining ingredients. Spoon into tubs.

Fennel, pasta and mushroom salad

It is a good idea to cook too much pasta when you are having it as a starter or main meal and then store the leftover pasta in the fridge or freezer until required for salads.

2 large heads fennel, sliced
3 tablespoons frozen peas
4 oz (115g) wholemeal pasta shapes
sea salt
1 teaspoon olive oil
6 oz (170g) button mushrooms, quartered
4 tablespoons mayonnaise

Good source of fibre with vitamin B complex.

1. Blanch the fennel in boiling water for 4 minutes. Add the peas, return to the boil and cook for a further 1½–2 minutes. Drain and leave to cool.
2. Cook the pasta in plenty of boiling salted water with the olive oil.
3. When the pasta is just tender to the bite, or *al dente*, remove from the heat and leave to cool.
4. Toss with the blanched vegetables, mushrooms and mayonnaise.

Fruit and nut case

Fresh or dried dates can be used in this recipe and any kind of nuts can be substituted for the peanuts. Try with cashews, pecans or pistachios.

1 green skinned eating apple, cored and diced
1 tablespoon lemon juice
3 oz (85g) seedless grapes, cut in half
2-inch (5cm) piece cucumber, diced
½ red pepper, seeded and diced
1 tablespoon chopped dates
1 tablespoon raisins
3 tablespoons raw peanuts
2 tablespoons sunflower seed oil

1. Plunge the diced apple into the lemon juice as soon as it is prepared. Toss well together to make sure that all the cut surfaces are coated with the juice.
2. Add all the remaining ingredients. Toss again and spoon into tubs.

Peanuts

Peanuts are rich in the B complex vitamins, particularly B_1 and niacin.

Pink pasta pot

4 oz (115g) wholemeal macaroni elbows
sea salt
2 teaspoons olive oil
1 raw beetroot
2 spring onions, finely chopped
a little grated orange rind
6 tablespoons thick yogurt or soured cream
freshly ground black pepper

1. Cook the pasta in plenty of boiling salted water with 1 teaspoon of olive oil.
2. When the pasta is just tender to the bite or *al dente*, drain and mix with the remaining olive oil. Leave to cool.
3. Grate the beetroot and mix with all the remaining ingredients. Pour over the pasta and toss well together.

Shropska

This popular salad comes from south east Europe. It makes a little meal in a tub. Top with a folded damp paper napkin or kitchen paper to stop the cheese drying out.

4 sticks celery
1 green pepper
1 very small onion
3-inch (7.5cm) piece cucumber
4 firm tomatoes
juice of 1 lemon
freshly chopped marjoram
6 oz (170g) Cheddar cheese, grated

1. Coarsely chop all the vegetable ingredients and toss in lemon juice. Add the marjoram and spoon into 4 tubs.
2. Top with grated cheese and seal.

Ginger and bean salad with brown rice

3 oz (85g) brown rice
7 fl oz (200ml) water
sea salt
2 teaspoons grated fresh root ginger
3 oz (85g) French, green or runner beans, stringed and cut into lengths
6 spring onions, finely chopped
2 tablespoons olive oil
1 teaspoon cider vinegar

Good carbohydrate and fibre plus vitamin B complex and vitamin C.

1. Place the brown rice, water and salt in a pan and bring to the boil. Stir once, cover with a lid, reduce the heat and simmer for 20–25 minutes until all the liquid has been absorbed and the rice is tender.
2. Stir in the grated root ginger and leave to cool.
3. Stir in all the remaining ingredients and toss together well.

Variation:

For a change add a few drops of sesame oil to this salad and top with a teaspoonful of toasted sesame seeds.

Macaroni mix

5 oz (140g) wholemeal macaroni elbows
a little salt
juice of half lemon
1 carrot, peeled and coarsely grated
8 radishes, trimmed and sliced
2 tablespoons raisins or sultanas
2 oz (55g) walnut halves, chopped
4 oz (115g) Edam cheese, diced
4 tablespoons Whole egg mayonnaise (see page 49)
2 tablespoons freshly chopped parsley

Almost a meal by itself, this recipe has good carbohydrate and fibre content plus protein and mixed vitamins.

1. Cook the macaroni in plenty of lightly-salted water for as long as directed on the pack.
2. Drain well and toss in lemon juice. Leave to cool.
3. Add all the remaining ingredients and mix together well.

Variation:

Try making the mayonnaise with 1-2 tablespoons of the salad oil replaced by walnut oil. This gives an unusually nutty flavour which complements the other ingredients well.

Serving suggestion:

Pack for lunch with Spicy tofu slices (see page 116).

Peanut and grape salad

2 dessert apples
1 tablespoon lemon juice
4 large sticks celery
4 oz (115g) green grapes, halved and seeded
4 oz (115g) fresh or toasted peanuts
4 tablespoons Whole egg mayonnaise (see page 49)
1 tablespoon peanut butter

1. Core and dice the unpeeled dessert apples and toss in lemon juice.
2. Add the celery, grapes and peanuts.
3. Blend the mayonnaise gradually into the peanut butter. Pour on the salad and toss together well.

N.B. If the fat content of this recipe is too high for you substitute Greek yogurt for the mayonnaise.

Cut and come again

Cheese, onion and pepper loaf

This is rich enough to serve as a main course with a salad.

½ red pepper, seeded and finely chopped
½ green pepper, seeded and finely
  chopped
1 small onion, finely chopped
2 oz (55g) butter or firm polyunsaturated
  margarine
6 oz (170g) Tilsit or Gouda cheese, grated
2 oz (55g) raw peanuts, chopped
3 eggs, beaten
sea salt and freshly ground black pepper

1. Set the oven to 190°C/375°F (Gas Mark 5).
2. Very gently fry the peppers and onion in the butter or margarine to soften them. This may take 3–4 minutes.
3. Place the flour, cheese and nuts in a bowl and add the vegetables. Stir and beat in the eggs and seasoning.
4. Pour into a 1 lb (455g) loaf tin and bake for 30 minutes. Leave to cool in the tin for 10 minutes and then transfer to a wire rack.
5. Turn out and cut into thickish slices.

Self-raising flour

To turn plain flour into self-raising flour add 2½ teaspoons baking powder to 8 oz (225g) plain flour.

Nut and mushroom terrine

To dress this dish up for a party buffet, turn out and decorate with bay-leaves or sliced gherkins and then coat in agar-agar jelly. Set any jelly that is left in a basin and chop to surround the terrine.

1½ lb (680g) mushrooms
2 onions, peeled and finely chopped
2 cloves garlic, crushed
3 tablespoons olive oil
4 oz (115g) ground almonds
4 oz (115g) ground cashew nuts
2 oz (55g) fresh wholemeal breadcrumbs
2 eggs
2 tablespoons freshly chopped parsley
2 teaspoons dried oregano
½ teaspoon dried thyme
1 teaspoon tomato ketchup
a few drops Tabasco sauce
sea salt and freshly ground black pepper

Good fibre and mixed vitamin content.
Serve with a fish salad to make up for the
low vitamin C content.

1. Set the oven to 180°C/350°F (Gas Mark 4).
2. Gently fry the mushrooms, onions and garlic in the cooking oil until soft. This may take up to 10 minutes or so
3. Mix with all the remaining ingredients seasoning well.
4. Spoon into a terrine dish and bake in a roasting tin filled with 1 inch (2.5cm) boiling water for 1 hour. Leave to cool before turning out and slicing.

Pissaladière

8 oz (225g) plain wholemeal flour
½ teaspoon salt
½ sachet easy bake yeast
1 tablespoon olive oil
4 fl oz (115ml) warm water
1½ lb (680g) onions, peeled and sliced
3 tablespoons olive oil (for frying onions)
1 clove garlic, crushed
1 teaspoon dried thyme
sea salt and freshly ground black pepper
1 tablespoon miso
1 lb (455g) tomatoes
1 oz (30g) black olives, stoned and sliced

Good source of fibre and B complex vitamin plus some vitamin E.

1. Sift the flour and salt into a bowl, adding back the bran from the sieve. Stir in the yeast.
2. Mix the oil and water and pour into a well in the centre of the flour. Work into a dough. Turn onto a floured board and knead for 8–10 minutes until smooth and elastic. Leave in a warm place for about an hour to rise to double in size.
3. Meanwhile make the filling by frying the onions in olive oil until pale golden in colour. This takes about 3–4 minutes.
4. Remove from the heat and stir in the garlic, thyme, seasoning and miso.
5. Set the oven to 190°C/375°F (Gas Mark 5). Knead the dough again briefly and roll out to line the base of a Swiss roll tin. Spread the onion mixture over the top.
6. Top with sliced tomatoes and olives and bake for 30–35 minutes. Leave to cool and cut into squares.

Mixed vegetable terrine

If you regularly have problems making a smooth white sauce, simply switch from a wooden spoon to a wire whisk and your problems will be over

4–6 small carrots, peeled
2 small courgettes, trimmed
2 oz (55g) French beans
½ red pepper, seeded
2 oz (55g) butter
2 oz (55g) flour
½ pint (285ml) skimmed milk
8 oz (225g) low-fat soft cheese
2 eggs, beaten
sea salt and freshly ground black pepper

1. Set the oven to 190°C/375°F (Gas Mark 5). Line a loaf tin or terrine dish with greased paper.
2. Steam the carrots for 15 minutes and the remaining vegetables for 10 minutes. Keep on one side.
3. Melt the butter in a pan and stir in the flour and milk. Bring to the boil stirring all the time. Cook for 2 minutes.
4. Remove from the heat and stir in all the remaining ingredients. Leave to cool a little.
5. Layer this sauce with the whole cooked vegetables in the loaf or terrine dish.
6. Cover with foil and bake in a roasting tin filled with 1 inch (2.5cm) hot water for about an hour until set. Leave to cool. Turn out and serve in slices.

N.B. Wholemeal flour can be used in this recipe, but the dish looks prettier if it is made with white or 83 per cent extraction flour.

Stuffed eggs

These eggs are both easy and popular to pack. Sandwich two halves together and carefully arrange in a plastic container.

6 eggs
2 tablespoons mayonnaise
1 teaspoon mild curry powder
1 tablespoon freshly chopped coriander
2 spring onions, finely chopped

1. Hard boil the eggs and leave to cool. Shell the eggs and cut in half lengthways. Scoop out all the yolks and mix with all the remaining ingredients. Spoon back into the hollows of the eggs and spread across the white as well so that when two halves are placed together there is a sandwich effect.

Stuffed spinach parcels

This unusual finger food makes a good addition to an elegant picnic or it can be served as part of a finger buffet or medley of canapés. In the latter case make the parcels just a little smaller.

16 medium-sized tender spinach leaves
  with stalks removed
4 eggs, beaten
4 tablespoons water
knob of butter
2 tomatoes, chopped
3 spring onions, finely chopped
sea salt and freshly ground black pepper

Good source of B complex vitamins plus some vitamin E.

1. Blanch the spinach leaves by plunging into boiling water and then immediately into cold water. Drain well.
2. Scramble the eggs with the water and butter, stirring until lightly set. Leave to cool.
3. Mix with the tomatoes and spring onions and season to taste.
4. Place a spoonful of the mixture on one end of each spinach leaf and roll up into a small cigar shaped parcel. Pack into boxes to transport for the picnic.

Tortilla squares

The easiest way to turn over the tortilla is to place a large plate over the pan and turn the tortilla onto it. Then slide back into the pan.

1 large potato, peeled and diced
1 medium onion, peeled and sliced
3 tablespoons olive oil
6 eggs, beaten
sea salt and freshly ground black pepper

Good source of vitamin B complex.

Variation:

Slivers of red and green peppers can be included in the vegetable mix for a change.

1. Fry the potato and onions in the oil in a non-stick frying pan over a medium heat for 15 minutes, turning occasionally. Do not allow the vegetables to brown
2. Beat the eggs and seasoning together and pour over the vegetables. Stir well and then leave over a low heat.
3. After about 5–6 minutes the base should be cooked. Turn over and continue cooking for a further 5–6 minutes until just cooked through.
4. Leave to cool and cut into squares. Wrap in cling-film and pack for a picnic.

Spicy tofu slices

10 oz (285g) block tofu
2 tablespoons finely grated carrot
1 tablespoon very finely chopped spring onion
1 teaspoon grated fresh root ginger
1 tablespoon roasted and ground sesame seeds
1 tablespoon roasted and ground sunflower seeds
sea salt and freshly ground black pepper
sunflower oil, for frying

1. Mash the tofu with a fork and mix with all the remaining ingredients except the oil.
2. Knead the mixture for 2–3 minutes until the dough is smooth and holds together. Shape into eight flat cakes.
3. Pour plenty of oil into a shallow frying pan and heat. Float cakes in the oil and fry for 3–4 minutes on each side until crisp. Drain on kitchen paper. Leave to cool on a wire rack.

Cucumber and tomato cheesecake

This cheesecake also looks very good on a buffet, decorated with fresh basil leaves.

10 unsweetened wholemeal biscuits
1½ oz (45g) butter or firm polyunsaturated margarine, melted
8 oz (225g) cottage cheese
1×8 oz (225g) tin tomatoes
1 tablespoon tomato purée
6 tablespoons dry white wine or vegetable stock
1 small cucumber or 3-inch (7.5cm) piece cucumber, grated
2 tablespoons freshly chopped basil
sea salt and freshly ground black pepper
2 teaspoons Gelozone

Good source of vitamin B complex plus vitamins A and E.

1. Crush the biscuits and mix with the melted fat. Press well down into the base of a 7-inch (17.5cm) loose-based cake tin. Place in the fridge to set.
2. Place the cottage cheese, the contents of the tin of tomatoes and the tomato purée in a food processor or blender and mix together well.
3. Transfer to a saucepan and add wine or stock, grated cucumber and basil and season to taste. Sprinkle on the *Gelozone* and bring to the boil, whisking all the time.
4. Leave to cool a little and pour over the biscuit base. Leave to cool and set in the fridge.
5. Take the cheesecake out of the tin and cut into wedges. Pack with a pasta pot or macaroni mix without the cheese.

Celeriac and swede flan

6 oz (170g) wholemeal shortcrust pastry
6 oz (170g) celeriac, peeled and grated
2 oz (55g) swede, peeled and grated
3 oz (85g) Cheddar cheese, grated
2 eggs, beaten
4 tablespoons milk
sea salt and freshly ground black pepper

Good source of fibre plus vitamin B complex.

1. Set the oven to 200°C/400°F (Gas Mark 6).
2. Roll out the pastry and use to line a 7-inch (17.5cm) shallow flan tin.
3. Mix the grated vegetables with the cheese. Mix all the remaining ingredients together and then mix with the vegetables and cheese.
4. Spoon into the pastry case and bake for about 1 hour until the flan is set in the centre and lightly browned.

Variation:

Tofu can be used in place of the cheese and soya milk in place of ordinary milk.

5
TREATS
AND SWEETS

Savoury specials

Broccoli and goat's cheese soufflé

3 oz (85g) broccoli florets
1 oz (30g) butter
1½ oz (45g) wholemeal flour
½ pint (285ml) skimmed milk
3 oz (85g) goat's cheese, with the rind
  removed, cut into pieces
4 eggs, separated
freshly ground black pepper
pinch nutmeg

1. Set the oven to 190°C/375°F (Gas
   Mark 5).
2. Steam the broccoli florets until just
   tender. Chop finely and keep on one
   side.
3. Heat the butter in a pan and stir in the
   flour and milk. Stir until the mixture
   thickens and boils. Cook for 2–3
   minutes.
4. Remove from the heat and add the
   broccoli, cheese, egg yolks, seasoning
   and nutmeg.
5. Whisk the egg whites until stiff and stir
   1 tablespoonful into the cheese mixture.
   Fold in the rest of the egg whites.
6. Spoon into four individual soufflé dishes
   or one large one and bake for 30–45
   minutes depending on size.

Spinach and tomato roulade

Use any kind of thick vegetable purée to flavour the filling in this party centrepiece. Ideas include celeriac, Jerusalem artichokes or parsnip.

1 lb (455g) spinach, washed
1½ oz (45g) butter
1½ oz (45g) 83 per cent extraction flour
6 fl oz (170ml) skimmed milk
sea salt and freshly ground black pepper
¼ teaspoon nutmeg
3 eggs, separated

Filling:

4 tomatoes, peeled and seeded and
  chopped
1 tablespoon tomato purée
5 oz (140g) low-fat soft cheese, quark or
  fromage frais

*Good source of vitamin B complex
including folic acid plus vitamins A, D and
E and iron.*

1. Set the oven to 190°C/375°F (Gas Mark 5). Line a Swiss roll tin with non-stick paper.
2. Place the spinach in a pan, cover with a lid and cook over a medium heat for 3–4 minutes until the spinach is limp. Drain very well, dry on kitchen paper and chop finely.
3. Heat butter, flour and milk in a pan. Bring to the boil, stirring all the time. The sauce should be quite thick.
4. Stir in the spinach, seasoning, nutmeg and egg yolks. Whisk the egg whites until they are very stiff and add a tablespoonful to the spinach mixture. Fold in the rest of the whites.
5. Spread the mixture smoothly over the prepared Swiss roll tin and bake for 20 minutes.
6. Prepare the filling by mixing the tomatoes and tomato purée with the soft cheese. Spoon into a pan and heat gently.
7. Cover a wire rack with a tea towel and turn the roulade on to this. Remove the paper and spread with the prepared filling.
8. Holding the tea towel in both hands roll up the roulade like a Swiss roll. Slice to serve.

Crespelle with fennel and peas

If using wholemeal flour it is best to use 83 per cent extraction or sift out some of the bran. You can use 100 per cent but the pancakes are a little heavy.

Crespelle:

2 oz (55g) plain flour (preferably 83 per cent extraction)
1 egg, beaten
¼ pint (140ml) skimmed milk
sea salt and freshly ground black pepper
polyunsaturated cooking oil

Filling:

1 large or 2 small heads fennel
2 tablespoons frozen peas
4 oz (115g) Ricotta or cottage cheese
pinch mixed herbs
sea salt and freshly ground black pepper

Sauces:

14 oz (395g) tin tomatoes
1 onion, sliced
freshly ground black pepper

½ pint (285ml) skimmed milk
1 small onion, sliced
1 carrot, sliced
1 bay-leaf
1½ oz (45g) butter or polyunsaturated margarine
1 oz (30g) Parmesan cheese, grated

1. Beat the flour with the egg and half the milk and then add the rest of the milk and the seasoning.
2. Lightly grease a small non-stick frying pan and use the batter to make eight small crespelle (pancakes).
3. Steam the fennel until just tender and chop finely. Let it cool and mix with the peas, cheese, herbs and seasoning. Use to fill the pancakes and roll into parcels.
4. Empty the tinned tomatoes into a pan and add the onion and pepper. Bring to the boil and simmer for 30 minutes.
5. Heat the milk in another pan and add the rest of the vegetables and the bay-leaf. Leave to stand until required, then strain and use to make a white sauce with the flour and fat. Whisk until the sauce thickens and then season to taste.
6. Set the oven to 200°C/400°F (Gas Mark 6). To put the dish together line the base of an entrée dish with three quarters of the tomato sauce. Place the filled crespelle on top and add the rest of the tomato sauce. Cover with the white sauce and sprinkle with Parmesan.
7. Bake for 20 minutes until lightly browned on top.

Courgettes in lemon cheese mousse

The salting is necessary to remove excess water from the courgettes. However, it is quite easy to wash most of it off.

12 oz (340g) courgettes, trimmed and
   sliced lengthways
sea salt
4 oz (115g) low-fat soft cheese
4 oz (115g) Cheddar cheese
2 eggs
grated rind of 1 lemon
freshly ground black pepper

*Good source of vitamin B complex and
vitamins A and D.*

1. Set the oven to 180°C/350°F (Gas
   Mark 4) and line a 1 lb (455g) loaf tin
   with non-stick baking paper, lightly
   greased.
2. Place the courgettes in a colander and
   sprinkle liberally with salt. Leave to
   stand for half an hour. Rinse under
   plenty of cold water. Drain and dry on
   kitchen paper.
3. Mix all the remaining ingredients in a
   bowl. Layer the mixture with the
   courgettes in the loaf tin, finishing with a
   layer of the cheese and lemon mixture.
   Bake in a roasting tin filled with 1 inch
   (2.5cm) hot water for 40 minutes. Turn
   out and slice to serve.

Serving suggestion:

Serve hot or cold as a starter or main
course dish with bulghur, rice or potatoes.

Italian crostini

This quantity will serve four people as an appetizer or 18 people (with one each) as finger
food. It will stretch to larger numbers if spread on smaller canapé bases.

1 long stick wholemeal French bread, cut
   into 18 pieces, toasted

1. Make the mushroom topping by frying
   the onion and garlic in hot oil for 3–4
   minutes until lightly-browned. Add the
   mushrooms and continue to fry until

Mushroom and garlic topping:

1 onion, peeled and finely chopped
2 cloves garlic, crushed
3 tablespoons olive oil
6 oz (170g) open mushrooms, finely
  chopped
2 tablespoons ground almonds
½ teaspoon fresh thyme or ¼ teaspoon
  dried
freshly ground black pepper

Tomato and carrot topping:

½ small onion, peeled and chopped
1 tablespoon olive oil
4 oz (115g) grated carrot
1×1¼ lb (565g) tin tomatoes, drained
2 sprigs fresh basil, chopped or ½
  teaspoon dried oregano
1 teaspoon tomato ketchup
salt and freshly ground black pepper

Goat's cheese topping:

3 oz (85g) firm goat's cheese, chopped
1½ oz (45g) walnuts, coarsely chopped
2 sprigs fresh tarragon or 1 teaspoon dried
  tarragon
2 tablespoons olive oil

soft. Stir in the nuts, herbs and pepper
and leave to cool.
2. Make the tomato and carrot topping by
   frying the onion in the oil for 5–6
   minutes until well-browned. Add all the
   remaining ingredients and bring to the
   boil. Cook over a medium heat, stirring
   from time to time until all the liquid has
   been absorbed.
3. Make the cheese topping by mixing all
   the ingredients together in a bowl.
4. Spread each topping on six pieces of the
   toast.

*Quite good fibre content with a reasonable
mix of vitamins. Serve fruit to follow to
make up the lack of vitamin C.*

Vegetable gâteau

This dish is equally good hot or cold.

8 oz (225g) celeriac
8 oz (225g) carrots
large head fennel
8 oz (225g) courgettes
2 oz (55g) soft butter
2 oz (55g) flour
½ pint (285ml) skimmed milk
8 oz (225g) low-fat soft cheese
2 eggs, beaten
sea salt and freshly ground black pepper
2 tablespoons flaked almonds

Good source of vitamin B complex and fibre.

1. Set the oven to 190°C/375°F (Gas Mark 5) and grease and line the base of an 8-inch (20cm) loose-based cake tin.
2. Cook the vegetables in a very little water or steamer until just tender. Leave to cool.
3. Melt the butter in a saucepan and whisk in the flour and milk. Bring to the boil whisking all the time. Cook for 2 minutes.
4. Remove from the heat and stir in the cheese, eggs, and seasonings. Leave to cool just a little.
5. Slice the vegetables. Arrange the celeriac in a layer in the base of the cake tin. Spread some sauce over the top. Next, add a layer of carrot and some more sauce.
6. Continue adding layers of vegetables and sauce until all the vegetables are used up. Finish with a layer of sauce.
7. Sprinkle with flaked almonds and bake for 1 hour and 15 minutes.
8. Remove from the cake tin before serving and cut into wedges.

N.B. The courgettes will cook more quickly than the other vegetables.

Leek and hazelnut loaf

2 large parsnips or 1 celeriac
1 onion, finely chopped
1 clove garlic, crushed
2 tablespoons sunflower or safflower oil
8 oz (225g) ground hazelnuts
4 oz (115g) fresh wholemeal breadcrumbs
1 egg, beaten
3 tablespoons redcurrant jelly
¼ pint (140ml) vegetable stock *or* ½
   teaspoon yeast extract and ¼ pint
   (140ml) water
1 tablespoon freshly chopped parsley
½ teaspoon freshly chopped rosemary
pinch of thyme
sea salt and freshly ground black pepper
1 lb (455g) leeks, trimmed and sliced
4 oz (115g) mushrooms, sliced

Very good source of fibre plus vitamin B complex, particularly B_1 and B_5, and vitamin E.

1. Brush a 2 lb (900g) non-stick loaf tin with oil and set the oven to 180°C/350°F (Gas Mark 4).
2. Cook the parsnips or celeriac in a very little water or in a steamer. Mash and leave to cool a little.
3. Fry the onion and garlic in one tablespoon of the oil until lightly browned. This will take 5–6 minutes. Stir in the nuts, breadcrumbs, egg and parsnips.
4. Mix the redcurrant jelly with the stock, herbs and seasonings and stir in the mixture. Keep on one side.
5. Fry the leeks and mushrooms in the remaining oil for 2–3 minutes to soften.
6. Spoon half the hazelnut mixture into the loaf tin and cover with the leeks and mushrooms. Add the rest of the hazelnut mixture and smooth over.
7. Bake for 1 hour. Leave to stand for 5 minutes before turning out, slicing and serve with Orange beetroot (see page 126).

Variations:

This loaf works very well with any kind of ground nuts. Simply change the herb flavouring to suit the new ingredients. Tarragon, for example, goes well with cashew nuts, and chervil with almonds.

N.B. If you do not have a non-stick loaf tin, line your tin with Bakewell paper.

Orange beetroot

1 tablespoon hazelnut oil
grated rind of 1 orange
12 oz (340g) cooked beetroot, coarsely
  grated

Good source of vitamin B complex.

1. Heat the hazelnut oil in a wok or deep frying pan.
2. Add the beetroot and orange rind and toss together over a high heat until heated through. Serve with the Leek and hazelnut loaf (see previous recipe).

Carrot and asparagus moulds

1 lb (455g) carrots, peeled and sliced into
  rounds
2 eggs, beaten
1 tablespoon plain wholemeal flour
2 fl oz (60ml) milk
1 teaspoon freshly chopped tarragon
sea salt and freshly ground black pepper
1×12 oz (340g) tin asparagus tips, drained

Garnish:

sprigs of fresh tarragon

Variations:

Any kind of root or firm vegetable can be used here. Try kohlrabi flavoured with chervil or celeriac flavoured with parsley.

1. Set the oven to 180°C/350°F (Gas Mark 4)
2. Cook the carrots in a very little boiling water or in a steamer. Drain, keeping the cooking liquor for stock.
3. Place 3 oz (85g) of the carrots on one side. Purée the rest in a blender or food processor with the eggs, flour, milk, herbs and seasoning.
4. Dry the asparagus on kitchen paper and arrange half in the base of four ramekin dishes. Place a slice of carrot in the centre of each one. Spoon a little of the carrot and egg mixture on top.
5. Next add a layer of sliced carrot, then another layer of the egg mixture and then a layer of asparagus. Finish off with a final layer of carrot and egg.
6. Place the ramekins in a roasting tray filled with 1 inch (2.5cm) hot water and bake for 60–70 minutes until the moulds are set. Turn out and serve garnished with sprigs of fresh tarragon.

Cauliflower terrine

If you don't want to use soured cream, use yogurt mixed with a teaspoon of cornflour.

1 cauliflower, trimmed
1 onion, peeled and finely chopped
knob of polyunsaturated margarine or a
  little cooking oil
3 oz (85g) fresh wholemeal breadcrumbs
¼ pint (140ml) soured cream
grated nutmeg
sea salt and freshly ground black pepper
2 eggs, beaten

1. Set the oven to 190°C/375°F (Gas
   Mark 5) and grease a terrine or soufflé
   dish.
2. Steam the cauliflower in a very little
   water or in a steamer (keep the liquid
   for stock for the following recipe). Mash
   the cooked cauliflower.
3. Fry the onion in the margarine or
   cooking oil for 4–5 minutes until very
   lightly browned. Mix with the mashed
   cauliflower and all the remaining
   ingredients.
4. Spoon the mixture into the prepared
   dish and bake for 1 hour. Sprinkle with
   freshly chopped parsley and serve with
   Provence-style corn (see recipe below).

Provence-style corn

Cut any large baby corn lengthways to speed the cooking time. Use the vegetable water from
the Cauliflower terrine recipe for the stock.

1 teaspoon olive oil
12 oz (340g) small baby corn
6 oz (170g) flat green beans or runner
  beans, stringed and cut into lengths
6 oz (170g) carrots, peeled and sliced
½ teaspoon dried Provence mixed herbs
3 tablespoons vegetable stock

1. Heat the oil in a large pan and quickly
   stir-fry the vegetables for 1–2 minutes.
2. Add the herbs and stock and reduce the
   heat to medium. Cook and stir until the
   liquid has evaporated and the vegetables
   are *al dente*. This only takes about 3–4
   minutes.
3. Serve with the Cauliflower terrine (see
   previous recipe).

Stuffed Chinese cabbage leaves

12 Chinese cabbage leaves

Filling:

1 large onion, peeled and chopped
2 sticks celery, chopped
1 tablespoon cooking oil
4 oz (115g) cream cheese
2 oz (55g) ground hazelnuts
4 oz (115g) cooked brown rice
1×8 oz (225g) tin bamboo shoots, chopped
1 tablespoon freshly chopped parsley
1-2 tablespoons vegetable stock
sea salt and freshly ground black pepper

Sauce:

½ pint (285ml) orange juice
2 tablespoons soya sauce
1 tablespoon cider vinegar
1 tablespoon grated root ginger
¼ teaspoon five spice powder

Good source of fibre and vitamin B complex.

1. Soften the Chinese leaves in boiling water. Leave to stand for 6-8 minutes.
2. Meanwhile fry the onion and celery in the cooking oil to soften them.
3. Remove from the heat and add all the remaining filling ingredients, with sufficient stock to give a firm but soft consistency.
4. Drain the Chinese leaves and dry with kitchen paper. Use the filling mixture to stuff the leaves. Roll up and secure with cocktail sticks. Place in a deep frying pan with a lid.
5. Mix all the sauce ingredients together and pour over the leaves.
6. Cover with the lid and bring to the boil. Reduce the heat and simmer for 15-20 minutes.

Serving suggestion:

Serve with Carroty noodles (see page 92).

Vegetarian phyllo pastry parcels _____

8 oz (225g) Feta cheese, crumbled
4 oz (115g) cottage cheese
4 oz (115g) frozen chopped spinach,
  thawed and pressed dry
pinch dried thyme
a little nutmeg
sea salt and freshly ground black pepper
6 sheets phyllo pastry
3 oz (85g) melted butter

1. Heat the oven to 220°C/425°F (Gas
   Mark 7).
2. Mix together the two cheeses, spinach,
   herbs and seasonings and heat gently in
   a saucepan.
3. Cut two sheets of phyllo pastry in half
   lengthways. Brush with some of the
   melted butter and press them together to
   make two double sheets.
4. Place a triangle of the cheese and
   spinach mixture in one corner of each
   double pastry layer and fold over to
   make a triangle.
5. Fold again diagonally and continue until
   the triangle is well covered.
6. Repeat with the other phyllo sheets.
   Brush all over with the melted butter
   and place on a greased baking tray.
7. Bake for 15 minutes until crisp and
   golden.

Sweet tooth indulgences

Tropical fruit pavlova

Meringue made with muscovado sugar tends to be much more chewy than ordinary meringues. The nuts also give added interest.

3 egg whites
pinch cream of tartar
6 oz (170g) light muscovado sugar
1 oz (30g) flaked almonds or chopped walnuts

Filling:

¼ pint (140ml) double cream
3 passion fruit
1 mango
1 paw paw
2 kiwi fruit

N.B. The meringue should be stiff enough not to fall out of the bowl when turned upside down. Do not fill the meringue shell until the last moment or it will go soggy.

1. Set the oven to 130°C/250°F (Gas Mark ½).
2. Whisk the egg whites with the cream of tartar until foamy. Then gradually whisk in the sugar. Continue whisking until the mixture is really stiff.
3. Carefully fold in the almonds or walnuts. Spoon the meringue onto a tray lined with Bakewell paper and shape into a large round with a hollowed out centre.
4. Bake for about 1½–2 hours until the meringue is golden in colour and firm on the base. Leave to cool on a wire rack.
5. To make the filling whisk the cream until soft peaks form.
6. Cut the passion fruit in half and scrape out all the pulp and seeds and fold into the cream. Spoon into the hollow in the meringue.
7. Top with sliced mango, paw paw and kiwi fruit.

Wholemeal choux ring with gooseberry cream

This choux ring is much crisper than it would be if it was made with white flour and it does not rise quite so much. However, the flavour is excellent. You could use 83 per cent extraction flour rather than sifting the bran out of the wholemeal flour.

¼ pint (140ml) water
2 oz (55g) butter
2½ oz (70g) wholemeal flour, weighed
    after sifting out the bran
pinch of salt
2 eggs

Gooseberry cream:

1 lb (455g) very ripe gooseberries, topped
    and tailed
½ pint (285ml) Greek yogurt
a little honey to taste

1. Set the oven to 200°C/400°F (Gas Mark 6). Line a baking tray with Bakewell paper.
2. Heat the water and butter in a saucepan. When the mixture boils add the flour and salt and stir until the mixture comes away from the sides of the pan. Remove from the heat and beat in the eggs, one at a time.
3. Spoon or pipe into a ring on the prepared tray and bake for 45–50 minutes or until the ring is really crisp and dry. Leave on a wire rack to cool.
4. Rub the gooseberries through a sieve or purée in a blender. Fold in the yogurt and add honey if the mixture is too tart for you.

N.B. Any kind of soft fruit can be puréed and used in this way. An unusual filling is sieved bananas. Add a little lemon juice to this one to prevent any discoloration.

Pear and wine jelly

I used up a bottle of rather flat Gewürztraminer and the results were excellent, but any kind of well-flavoured wine can be used.

3 ripe pears, peeled, cored and diced
¾ pint (425ml) well-flavoured white wine
juice of 1 small lemon
water
2 teaspoons agar-agar

1. Place the pears in a flat entrée dish.
2. Pour the wine and lemon juice into a measuring jug and make up to 1 pint (570ml) with water. Pour into a saucepan and bring to the boil.
3. Add the agar-agar as directed on the pack and stir until dissolved. Pour onto the pears.
4. Leave to cool and set in the fridge.

Grapefruit cheesecake

Gelozone reacts to the acidity in citrus fruits and so you may need a little more *Gelozone* if you find it only sets very lightly.

10 wholemeal digestive biscuits, crushed
2 oz (55g) butter or firm polyunsaturated margarine, melted
4 grapefruits, segmented
8 oz (225g) cottage cheese
6 fl oz (170ml) grapefruit juice
2 teaspoons *Gelozone*

1. Mix the crushed biscuits with the melted fat and press into the base of an 8-inch (20cm) cake tin. Place in the fridge to set.
2. Remove all the pith and white membranes from the grapefruit and blend half in a blender with the cottage cheese and grapefruit juice.
3. Transfer to a small saucepan and sprinkle the *Gelozone* over the top. Bring to the boil. Stir and leave to cool a little.
4. Pour over the base in the cake tin. Place in the fridge to set.
5. Decorate the top with the remaining grapefruit segments.

Pashka

This used to be the traditional Easter cake in certain parts of Russia.

12 oz (340g) very dry curd cheese*
2 oz (55g) butter, softened
1 tablespoon set honey
2 oz (55g) yogurt
1 egg, beaten
2 oz (55g) chopped walnuts, hazelnuts or
almonds
2 oz (55g) raisins
2 oz (55g) finely chopped dried apricots
½ oz (15g) chopped candied peel
¼ teaspoon vanilla essence

Garnish:

toasted almonds

1. Beat the curd cheese with the butter and then gradually beat in all the remaining ingredients except the garnish.
2. Line a basin with muslin, leaving enough material to fold over the top. Spoon in the cheese mixture. Smooth the top and cover with muslin.
3. Place a weight on the top and leave for at least 12 hours.
4. Turn out of the basin and remove the cloth. Decorate with toasted almonds. Cut into wedges to serve.

* For really dry curd cheese, rub cottage cheese through a sieve and then hang up to drain in muslin for 2 hours.

All the year round fruit crumble

Use any fruit in season. Most fruit will not require any pre-cooking. Apples, gooseberries and pears are exceptions. Experiment with fruit combinations — good ideas include peaches and blueberries or bilberries and gooseberries and strawberries. This recipe is a good way to use up any fruit which is slightly damaged or bruised, for example, apples and figs, rhubarb and thinly sliced lemon, or plums and sliced pears.

1½–2 lb (680–900g) fresh fruit
sugar or honey to taste

Topping:

2 oz (55g) wholemeal flour
1 oz (30g) medium oatmeal or rolled oats
1 oz (30g) hazelnuts, chopped
2 oz (55g) butter, cut into small pieces
1½ oz (45g) dark muscovado sugar

1. Set the oven to 180°C/350°F (Gas Mark 4).
2. Slice the fruit and if necessary stew in a very little water. Add sugar or honey to taste and spoon into a pie dish.
3. Mix together the flour, oatmeal and nuts. Add the fat and rub in until the mixture resembles fine breadcrumbs.
4. Stir in the muscovado sugar and sprinkle over the top of the fruit. Bake for 30–35 minutes.

Prune soufflé

Sprinkle with toasted nuts just before serving as a variation or pour in a little orange liqueur.

4 oz (115g) dried prunes
boiling water
grated rind and juice of 1 orange
caster sugar, to taste
3 eggs, separated

1. Set the oven to 190°C/375°F (Gas Mark 5).
2. Soak the prunes by covering with boiling water and leaving to stand for 2 hours.
3. Cook in the water in which they were soaked for 5–6 minutes until tender. Drain and leave to cool a little.
4. Remove the stones and purée in a blender with the orange rind and juice. Add sugar to taste.
5. Mix in the egg yolks. Whisk the egg whites until they are really stiff. Stir a tablespoonful into the prune mixture and fold in the rest.
6. Spoon into individual ramekin dishes and bake for 30 minutes until set in the centre. Serve at once.

Lebanese pastries

2 oz (55g) wholemeal breadcrumbs
4 oz (115g) pistachio nuts, finely chopped
2 oz (55g) pine kernels, finely chopped
2 oz (55g) ground walnuts
6–8 tablespoons honey
6–8 sheets phyllo pastry
2 oz (55g) melted butter

1. Set the oven to 180°C/350°F (Gas Mark 4).
2. Toast the breadcrumbs under the grill until golden but do not allow them to burn. Mix with the nuts and honey.
3. Line a greased 7×11-inch (17×27cm) Swiss roll tin with 3–4 sheets of pastry, brushing each one with melted butter as you put them in place.
4. Spread the nut mixture over the pastry and then top with a second layer of 3–4 sheets of pastry and melted butter.
5. Bake for 35–40 minutes until crisp and golden. Cut into squares or fingers and serve in small quantities with Greek yogurt.

Marmalade fruit loaf

8 oz (225g) wholemeal self-raising flour
1 tablespoon home-made or old-fashioned Seville orange marmalade
2 tablespoons black treacle
2 tablespoons raisins
a little milk

1. Set the oven to 180°C/350°F (Gas Mark 4). Line a 1 lb (455g) loaf tin with baking paper.
2. Place the flour in a bowl. Make a well in the centre and add all the ingredients except the milk. Work to a stiffish dough using a little milk if necessary.
3. Spoon into the prepared tin and bake for 45 minutes. Turn out onto a wire rack and leave to cool.

Coffee and walnut buns

The buns are very good topped with coffee water icing and a walnut half.

3 oz (85g) butter
3 oz (85g) light muscovado sugar
1 egg, beaten
3 oz (85g) wholemeal flour
1 tablespoon milk and water
1 dessertspoon coffee essence
pinch of salt
½ teaspoon baking powder
1 oz (30g) chopped walnuts

1. Set the oven to 190°C/375°F (Gas Mark 5).
2. Cream the fat and sugar together until light and fluffy. Beat in the egg with a little of the flour, the milk and water and the coffee essence. Fold in the rest of the dry ingredients.
3. Spoon into paper bun cases and place on a baking tray. Bake for 6 minutes.
4. Reduce the heat to 150°C/300°F (Gas Mark 2) and cook for a further 5 minutes.

Chocolate gateau

This deliciously rich and moist chocolate cake can be filled with jam or chocolate butter icing. Top with sifted sugar or, for a very special occasion, coat with 4 oz (115g) chocolate, melted and mixed with 2 oz (55g) icing sugar, 2 dessertspoons sherry and 1 oz (30g) butter.

4 oz (115g) butter
4 oz (115g) light muscovado sugar
2 eggs, beaten
4 oz (115g) wholemeal self-raising flour
3 oz (85g) ground almonds
2 oz (55g) cocoa or carob powder
1 oz (30g) drinking chocolate (optional)
1 teaspoon coffee essence
1 dessertspoon sherry

1. Set the oven to 180°C/350°F (Gas Mark 4) and grease and line the base of a cake tin.
2. Cream the butter and sugar until light and fluffy. Beat in the eggs one at a time, adding a little flour in between them.
3. Mix the remaining flour with the almonds, cocoa or carob powder and drinking chocolate (if using). Fold into the mixture. Stir in the coffee essence and sherry.
4. Spoon into the prepared tin and bake for 70 minutes. Leave to cool a little and then transfer to a wire rack and cool completely.

Nutty flapjack

Any kind of breakfast cereals can be used in this recipe but it will be very sticky if you decrease the quantity of rolled oats.

6 oz (170g) butter
6 oz (170g) soft brown sugar
4 oz (115g) golden syrup
3 oz (85g) chopped mixed nuts
3 oz (85g) cornflakes
6 oz (170g) rolled oats

1. Set the oven to 190°C/375°F (Gas Mark 5). Line a 6×8-inch (15×20cm) tin with Bakewell paper.
2. Melt the butter and sugar in a pan. Do not allow to boil. Stir in all the remaining ingredients away from the heat.
3. Spoon the mixture into the prepared tin and spread out smoothly. Bake for 20 minutes.
4. Remove from the oven and cut into squares or fingers about 2–3 minutes later.
5. Leave to cool in the tin and then separate.

Date and malt loaf

Despite the absence of fat in the recipe this delicious loaf is moist enough to eat without spreading with butter or margarine.

3 oz (85g) malt extract
2 oz (55g) molasses or black treacle
6 fl oz (170ml) skimmed milk
8 oz (225g) wholemeal flour
2 teaspoons baking powder
¼ teaspoon salt
3 oz (85g) dried dates, stoned and chopped
1 egg, beaten

1. Set the oven to 190°C/375°F (Gas Mark 5) and grease a 1 lb (455g) loaf tin.
2. Heat the malt, syrup and milk in a saucepan over a gentle heat and beat until well blended. Remove from the heat.
3. Mix the flour, baking powder, salt and dates in a large bowl.
4. Add the beaten egg and the malt mixture, stirring all the time with a wooden spoon.
5. Pour the mixture into the prepared tin and bake for about 45 minutes until firm and a skewer comes out clean. Turn out to cool on a wire rack.

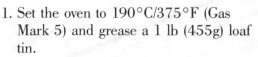

APPENDIX

Please note the following differences between the American and British cookery terms:

1 teaspoon (5ml)	1¼ teaspoon	Chinese leaves	Bok Choy, Chinese cabbage
1 tablespoon (15ml)	1¼ tablespoon		
1 pint (20 fl oz/570ml)	1¾ pints	coriander (fresh)	cilantro
8 fl oz (225ml)	1 cup	cornflour	corn starch
		courgettes	zucchini
		digestive biscuit	Graham cracker
almonds, flaked	slivered almonds	endive	chicory
aubergine	eggplant	frying pan	skillet
Bakewell/greaseproof paper	waxed paper	grill	broil(er)
		jelly	jello
beans: broad	fava beans	kitchen paper	paper towel
butter	lima beans	lettuce: corn	lamb's lettuce
French	snap beans	round	Bibb lettuce
haricot	navy beans	mangetout	snow peas
beetroot	beet	paw paw	papaya
bicarbonate of soda	baking soda	sieve	strain(er)
celeriac	celery knob/root	spring greens	collards
celery: head	bunch	spring onion	scallion
stalk	stick	starter	appetizer
cheese: cottage	pot cheese	swede	rutabaga
curd	ricotta or farmer's cheese	tomato purée	tomato paste
		walnuts	English walnuts
chick-peas	garbanzos	wholemeal	whole wheat
chicory	endive	yogurt, natural	plain yogurt

INDEX